Everyday Enterprise Architecture

Sense-making, Strategy, Structures, and Solutions

Tom Graves

Apress®

Everyday Enterprise Architecture: Sense-making, Strategy, Structures, and Solutions

Tom Graves
Eaglehawk, VIC, Australia

ISBN-13 (pbk): 978-1-4842-8903-7   ISBN-13 (electronic): 978-1-4842-8904-4
https://doi.org/10.1007/978-1-4842-8904-4

Managing Director, Apress Media LLC: Welmoed Spahr
Acquisitions Editor: Aditee Mirashi
Development Editor: James Markham
Coordinating Editor: Aditee Mirashi

Cover designed by eStudioCalamar

Cover image designed by Freepik (www.freepik.com)

Distributed to the book trade worldwide by Springer Science+Business Media New York, 1 New York Plaza, Suite 4600, New York, NY 10004-1562, USA. Phone 1-800-SPRINGER, fax (201) 348-4505, e-mail orders-ny@springer-sbm.com, or visit www.springeronline.com. Apress Media, LLC is a California LLC and the sole member (owner) is Springer Science + Business Media Finance Inc (SSBM Finance Inc). SSBM Finance Inc is a **Delaware** corporation.

For information on translations, please e-mail booktranslations@springernature.com; for reprint, paperback, or audio rights, please e-mail bookpermissions@springernature.com.

Apress titles may be purchased in bulk for academic, corporate, or promotional use. eBook versions and licenses are also available for most titles. For more information, reference our Print and eBook Bulk Sales web page at http://www.apress.com/bulk-sales.

Any source code or other supplementary material referenced by the author in this book is available to readers on GitHub via the book's product page, located at www.apress.com/978-1-4842-8903-7. For more detailed information, please visit http://www.apress.com/source-code.

Printed on acid-free paper

Table of Contents

About the Author

 **Tom Graves** has been an independent consultant for more than four decades, in business transformation, enterprise architecture, and knowledge management. His clients in Europe, Australasia, and the Americas cover a broad range of industries including banking, utilities, manufacturing, logistics, engineering, media, telecoms, research, defense, and government. He has a special interest in architectures beyond IT and integration between IT-based and non-IT-based services.

About the Technical Reviewer

 **Daljit Banger** has 38 years of solid IT industry experience, having undertaken assignments in locations across the globe – the UK, the United States, Sweden, Switzerland, Finland, Hong Kong, and Brazil to name but a few – on behalf of large multinational companies.

Daljit has successfully managed several large professional teams of architects, written in several publications, and is the author of several freeware software products for enterprise architecture.

Daljit holds a Master of Science (MSc) degree and is a Chartered IT Fellow of the British Computer Society (BCS) and chairs the BCS Enterprise Architecture Specialist Group.

Acknowledgments

Among others, the following people kindly provided comments, advice, suggestions, and feedback on various ideas expressed in this book: Sally Bean (Sally Bean Consulting, GB), Shawn Callahan (Anecdote, Australia), Pat Ferdinandi (SBDI, USA), Paul Jansen (Jansen, BE), Anders Østergaard Jensen (Sydney, Australia), John Polgreen (GTRA, USA), Chris Potts (Dominic Barrow, GB), Kevin Smith (Pragmatic, GB), Michael Smith (Latidos, MX), Richard Veryard (NPRI, GB).

Please note that, to preserve commercial and personal confidentiality, the stories and examples in this book have been adapted, combined, and in part fictionalized from experiences in a variety of contexts, and do not and are not intended to represent any specific individual or organization.

Trademarks or registered trademarks such as Cynefin, Zachman, TOGAF, etc., are acknowledged as the intellectual property of the respective owners.

Introduction

What exactly do we *do* every day in enterprise-architecture? What value does it deliver to the business? How do we develop our skills and experience, our judgment and awareness, so as to keep on enhancing the value that we deliver? And how do we do it *fast*, to respond to the real-time pressures of an always-on business world?

Many books on enterprise-architecture place an emphasis on frameworks, models, or methods – their overall *theory* of architecture, without much description of what actually happens in day-to-day practice. The reason for that gap is simple: if we start from theory, it's hard to show much more than guidelines and principles without getting lost in irrelevant detail, because every architecture context is different.

So this book takes almost the opposite approach. We concentrate on the everyday *activities* that underpin each of the architecture disciplines – particularly the core processes such as sensemaking and design-thinking.

We explore how and why and when the various items of "theory-stuff" come into the picture – all those methods, frameworks, models, metamodels, and other information-sources.

And we show how to do all of that in a real architecture-project that must deliver real business-value in just two working weeks – not the two years or more required by some other approaches to enterprise-architecture. So yes, *real* enterprise-architecture, in real-time, that really *does* make business sense.

Use the architecture itself to explain how to do enterprise architecture.

Illustrate it by tackling a real enterprise-level business problem.

Exactly ten days in which to do it.

Starting now.

Go.

Interested? Read on…

Who Should Read This Book?

The principles and practice described here apply to every type of enterprise – for-profit, not-for-profit, government, whatever – and at every scale, from a global corporation all the way down to the local school's sports-club. So in principle, and in practice too, it should be relevant to just about everyone.

This book should be especially useful for enterprise and business architects, but also for executives, strategists, strategic analysts, and any others who are tasked with understanding the enterprise as a whole.

Enterprise-architectures provide a "big-picture" overview for other architecture disciplines: so this would also be useful for process architects, security architects, solution architects, software architects, and the like.

What's in This Book?

The aim of this book is to show what *actually* needs to happen in enterprise-architecture practice – not just its outcomes, but the activities from which those outcomes arise. As part of this, the book introduces a new technique called "context-space mapping," which provides a structured method for sensemaking across the entire context of an enterprise. There's also a strong emphasis here on what building-architects describe as "meta-thinking" – the reflective "thinking about thinking" through which the quality of personal practice is developed.

The book and its content are built around a real two-week project explicitly undertaken to illustrate all of these themes. Each of the ten main chapters in the book describes the respective day's activities, and includes and expands on the actual project-diary entries for that day, which are shown as follows:

Diary-entries have their own distinct formatting to separate them from the main text

---

We'll use the project-diary for records, notes, sketch-diagrams, and anything else we'd need to document as we go along.

There are also various comments, anecdotes, asides, and examples – again drawn from real business practice – which are shown as follows:

A story, anecdote, or aside provides a real-world example of the point that's being discussed in the main text.

Most books on enterprise-architecture and the like will include many illustrative models and diagrams, and this too follows that tradition. What's different here is that many of these diagrams are adapted straight from the sketch-pad or whiteboard, to emphasize that this book is all about what happens in real-world practice.

There are actually two projects running in parallel during the two-week period described in this book:

- How to use architecture ideas and activities to describe what actually happens in a real enterprise-architecture project, and the business-reasons and business-value for each of those activities

...and, selected during the early stages of that main project, to illustrate each of the respective principles and practices:

- Using architecture to address a real enterprise-level business-problem that was a serious and urgent concern to one of our clients

The architecture activities for this second project are described in a separate section in the later part of each day's chapter.

Each of those chapters ends with another section that provides suggestions for how to apply the same principles in your own architecture work.

There are also two additional chapters after the overall projects. The first of these describes the structures of the information-repositories needed for enterprise-architecture, and summarizes the respective content for each. The second of these two chapters provides more detail on context-space mapping, with some additional examples of cross-maps that can be useful in specific types of sensemaking. And finally there's an appendix that lists the various resources referenced within the book.

That's the overall structure of what follows. But the clock's already ticking on this architecture-project: time to get started.

CHAPTER 1

Day 1: Getting Started

Whatever we do, however we approach it, and whichever part of the organization we work in, all of enterprise-architecture comes down to one single, simple idea:

Things work better when they work together, with clarity, with elegance, on purpose.

Enterprise-architects are responsible to the organization to make that happen: the underlying aim of every item of architecture-work in the enterprise is to make things work better for everyone, in a more effective way.

And every item of architecture-work should start from an explicit business-question. In this specific case, in exploring the role of architecture itself, the "business-question" will come from us, but the principle remains the same as for any other architecture task. So for here, the question is this:

What do enterprise-architects *do*?

And how exactly do they add value to the business?

One obvious driver for value to the business will be speed of response: the work is not going to be of much value if we allow ourselves to get stuck in "analysis-paralysis." But the business will also need us to deliver something that is of practical use: we do need to get the balance right here. So, following an Agile-style development principle, we'll pick an arbitrary but appropriate timescale – ten working-days, or two business-weeks – for a first-level architecture iteration. At the end of that time, we'll review and decide what to do next.

Action: *Start a project-diary*. Document the key requirements and decisions to date:

© Tom Graves 2023
T. Graves, *Everyday Enterprise Architecture*, https://doi.org/10.1007/978-1-4842-8904-4_1

Commitment
- use architecture methods, etc., to describe how to do architecture-development in real-time
- topic for the architecture-project is architecture itself
- document in book-form
- timescale: 10 working days
- success-criteria: better understanding of architecture purpose and practice

This means we're already in Day 1 for the project: no time to waste.

Overall Aim, Scope, and Purpose

As a starting-point, we briefly summarize some key themes and understandings about what this work will involve, and ideas about what we want to have achieved by the end of this cycle:

Starting-point:
- project-stakeholders are architects and architects' clients
- use the existing Agile-architecture development-process
- demonstrate the recursion, etc., within that process
- particularly want to describe the sensemaking and decision-making components of architecture, such as via context-space mapping

Action: *Identify the stakeholders and scope.* Every item of architecture work will apply to and affect one or more groups of stakeholders, so we need to identify who those are, as early as possible in the project. We describe these people as "stakeholders" rather than "clients," because although the work is usually *for* a specific group of people – such as you, in this case – there are often many others who will be affected *by* it, and whose feelings and opinions will definitely impact the overall effectiveness of the end-result. It's essential to set the right scope, so it's important to note that for architecture work, the scope of *influence* – the stakeholders whose views we need to take into account – is usually several steps broader than the scope of *action* – the part of the business for which we have the authority and budget to enact change.

Action: *Identify the methods and overall approach to be used.* The aim here is to use architecture to describe how architecture works, so we'll need to base the work on existing disciplines, frameworks, and methods. One key to this is the way in which

the same overall practices recur not just as sequential cycles, but within other cycles –
a pattern known as *recursion*. We also want to explore and explain the process of
sensemaking and decision-making that is the real core of architecture-practice.

Agile-architecture cycle:

1. Setup – context, scope, values, business-purpose, and success-criteria

2. Architecture-side: what do we have, what do we want, what's the difference from here to there

3. Implementation-side: what needs to change, what's the plan, do it

4. Wrap-up: what value was gained, what have we learnt, what's next

Include glossary/thesaurus, models, opportunity/risk, issues, etc.

Perhaps use an adapted version of TOGAF ADM to illustrate this?

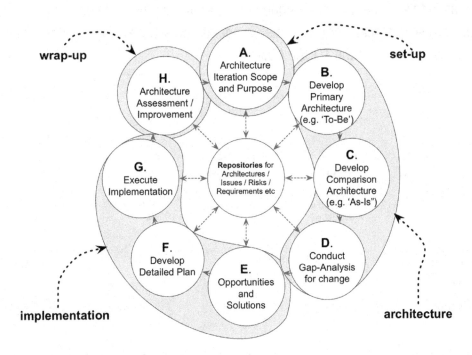

Figure 1-1. *The architecture cycle*

As in the project-diary, the architecture-development process is structured as a cycle
with four main groups of activities. As shown in Figure 1-1, we've adapted this from
the style established by the TOGAF ADM (The Open Group Architecture Framework
Architecture Development Method – see Appendix C), so we've laid out these four
groups into eight distinct phases:

- A setup phase

- A group of three phases on architecture-assessment

- Another group of three phases on implementing the results of that assessment

- And a shared completion-phase that wraps up the overall project

---

By the way, do note that what we're describing here is <u>not</u> the TOGAF ADM. It intentionally uses the same kind of layout, to support compatibility, but some of the differences are fundamental. In particular, phases B, C, and D work in a very different way: in TOGAF, these are arguably usable only for larger-scale IT projects, whereas in this frame they're designed for use with any type of content or context, any type of scope, scale, or timescale. To see the difference, compare the labels for each phase to those in the TOGAF ADM.

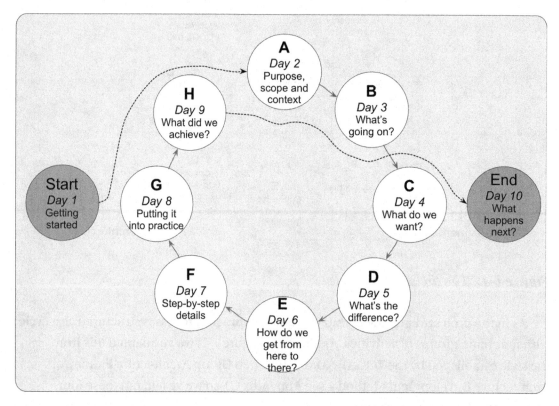

Figure 1-2. *Structure for this project: cycles within a cycle*

As shown in Figure 1-2, there will be just one main cycle for this project, with separate smaller cycles either side to provide lead-in (Start) and follow-up (End). Each of these cycles may well include other cycles within it, to support the needs for recursion.

In effect, this first day (labelled Start in Figure 1-2) is one very rapid skim through that cycle, looking at purpose, then the needs that arise from that purpose, and what we need to do to action those requirements, followed by a quick wrap-up and review. After that we'll do a full cycle, allocating one day to each set of activities (phases A to H). We'll then complete the project with a final overall review, which again will be another rapid one-day cycle (End).

Initial Aim, Scope, and Stakeholders

For this initial one-day cycle, the stakeholders are ourselves, the scope is the same "how would we describe architecture?" and the aim is to develop a plan of action for the remaining work that will deliver useful results in the small amount of time that we have.

Initial Assessment

Right at the start of an assessment-phase, by definition, we don't know what we're doing, and we don't know what to do. We know where we want to go, but not much more than that. This can often bring on a strong feeling of inadequacy, incompetence, even of failure, so it's important to realize that *this bewilderment is normal and to be expected at this stage of the process.*

For almost everyone, this kind of inherent uncertainty can be very uncomfortable. And although it takes a lot of practice to become "comfortable with being uncomfortable," that's a very useful skill for architects to develop, because our clients will be going through exactly the same experience, and we'll need to help them through it too. What helps most here is to acknowledge what we feel, yet remember to follow the process: keep the focus on the overall aim or "vision," and then *do something* – almost anything, in fact – to give appropriate ideas somewhere to begin to coalesce.

Action: *Don't fight against the uncertainty, work with it.* In this phase of the work, it's best to place ourselves in an "information-rich" environment of some kind, to provide the broadest possible range of triggers for ideas. For some people this will literally be "noisy" – music, crowds, the market – whilst others would prefer the library or a wild scatter of papers and images. The key is to keep a notepad or voice-recorder to hand at all times here, to catch the often-fleeting impressions that will start the ball rolling.

Assorted notes:

- start with a mind-map of key themes/concerns: what is "enterprise architecture"? for this purpose?
- how would I use this? – give a real example
- "what is an enterprise?" – what is "the enterprise" for this?
- use simple checklists: context-space; five-principles; five-elements; four-dimensions segments-model (extended-Zachman)

As shown in Figure 1-3, the free-form nature of mind-mapping can be useful here – if only to express how we feel about the uncertainty at this point...

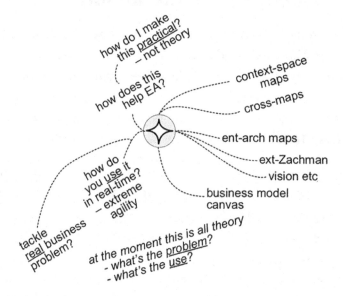

Figure 1-3. *Initial mind-map*

Importantly, *all* we are doing at this stage is assessment and information-gathering: we document the ideas and images that come up, but we *don't* take action to follow up on any of them as yet. This does, however, point to a key operating principle that we will use throughout the entire process:

Action: *If anything comes up during a project-phase that more properly fits the function of a later phase, the only action should be to document and tag it for retrieval during that later phase.* For example, that list in the preceding graphic includes "how would I use this?" and "use simple checklists" – both of which are more about action than assessment, so we do nothing more about them for now, other than ensure that we will remember them when we get to the "implementation" stage of this small cycle. But the question "what is an enterprise?" *is* useful for assessment, so we do need to explore that point briefly before moving on.

Perhaps unsurprisingly, the question "what is an enterprise?" is fundamental to enterprise-architecture. This is important because many discussions about enterprise-architecture will assume that it's solely about IT. The point here is that even if we're only concerned with IT, we still need to set its respective "enterprise" in a broader scope – *much* broader, in fact.

The key distinction here is that we develop an architecture *for* an organization, but *about* an enterprise that provides its context:

- The *organization* is bounded by *rules, roles, and responsibilities*
- The *enterprise* is bounded by *vision, values, and shared commitment*

This essential difference between rule-based versus values-based means that whilst we can sort-of control what happens within an organization, we can't do the same with an enterprise. The best we can do is negotiate agreements – which is a very different process than issuing organizational edicts...

An organization is also an enterprise in its own right, of course (though an enterprise is not necessarily an organization) – hence the common habit of describing a business-organization as "the enterprise." But for the context we'd typically need for an architecture, a useful guideline, as shown in Figure 1-4, is that *the enterprise in scope is at least three steps larger than the organization in scope.*

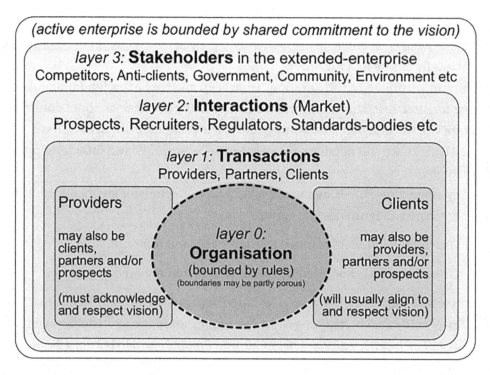

Figure 1-4. Organization and enterprise

For a business-organization, those three steps or layers outward would typically include:

- *Layer #0 (root)*: The organization itself

- *Layer #1 (transactions)*: Clients, suppliers, suppliers, service-providers, and partners

- *Layer #2 (interactions)*: Prospects, regulators, recruiters, the market, and more

- *Layer #3 (further stakeholders)*: Competitors, non-clients, anti-clients, government, community, environment, and more

For a government department or not-for-profit organization, we might use alternate labels for "clients," "prospects," or "competitors," but the overall structure would be much the same.

Another useful view here would be in terms of responsibilities, by using a crossmap of RACI (Responsible, Accountable, Consulted, Informed) onto that layered structure. For example, relative to the organization, as layer-0, we would see the following RACI relationships:

- *Layer #1 (transactions)*: Responsible/accountable with suppliers, customers, etc.

- *Layer #2 (interactions)*: Consulting and/or consulted by the market

- *Layer #3 (further stakeholders)*: Informing and/or informed by those further stakeholders

And we'll also see the same structure recurring at different levels *within* organizations. For example, in classic IT-oriented "enterprise"-architectures such as TOGAF, we would see the following layers:

- *Layer #0*: Physical IT – TOGAF "IT-Infrastructure Architecture"

- *Layer #1*: The "users" of the physical IT-infrastructure, namely, applications and data and their service or partner interfaces – TOGAF "Information-Systems Architectures"

- *Layer #2*: The clients of those applications, human or otherwise – a rather muddled part of TOGAF "Business Architecture"

- *Layer #3*: The "business ecosystem" for the overall architecture – the remainder of TOGAF "Business Architecture"

It's extremely useful to keep that layered pattern in mind at all times when doing any kind of enterprise-architecture.

Another useful tactic in this phase is to look outside of our own industry. Here, for example, we could turn to building-architecture and explore Matthew Frederick's checklist-style book *101 Things I Learned In Architecture School* (see Appendix C for more details on this and other books). From there, we could scribble into the project-diary some quick notes on various themes that caught the eye:

From the "101 Things" architecture-book:
- the *parti* is the central idea for the structure – what is the *parti* here?
- sense of place (and what goes on in that place)
- architecture vs. space-planning, engineering, design
- "good designers are fast on their feet" – an Agile view of the *parti*
- emphasis on process, not product
- importance of "thinking about thinking," as meta-methodology
- levels of knowing: simplicity, complexity, informed-simplicity
- design in section, not solely in plan! – views into "context-space"
- design with models – modeling as a sensemaking/design process
- gaining control of design process at first feels like losing control
- architecture an exercise in truth and in narrative – what is the story?
- everything is in context to a larger context – layering of "enterprise"
- design is constrained by rules, regulations, other people's priorities: use those constraints to encourage creativity
- do something to get started – and give it a name

Remember that there's no particular plan at this stage: it's just about creating a space in which ideas can arise, and then collating the results in re-usable form. It may be that in the end, we don't use some of these ideas at all: but at this stage, we not only don't know but *can't* know which ideas will or won't be of use. Yet placing these notes in the project-diary means that they'll be available to us if and when we need them: that's all we're doing here.

One idea from that list that's useful right now is the architectural notion of the "*parti.*" As Frederick puts it, "a *parti* is the central idea or concept of a building ... *parti* derives from understandings that are nonarchitectural and must be cultivated before architectural form can be born." It's unlikely to arrive just yet, but we need to keep our awareness open for any pointers to our own enterprise-architecture equivalents of the *parti* – a single unifying theme that will link all aspects of this architecture together.

It's not much work to do this, of course, but that's probably all the assessment that we need to do at this very early stage.

Initial Implementation

"Implementation" in this context will likewise be very simple: most of it is just an exploration and confirmation of the key tools that we would use in the main body of the work. For the main project here, these were listed in the earlier notes:

- Context-space mapping

- Five key principles from systems-theory

- Five-elements model of concurrent-lifecycle business processes

- Four-dimensions segments-model

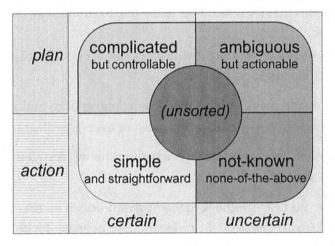

Figure 1-5. *Typical base-frame for context-space mapping*

Context-space mapping (CSM) is a method for using descriptive frameworks in architecture. The example we will use here adapts a framework called SCAN, that describes a context in terms of four distinct "domains" of interpretation and action (Figure 1-5).

Those four main "domains" within that diagram in effect represent distinct regions in a spectrum of low to high repeatability, or low to high abstraction, with Not-known at the low end and Simple at the high end. It's simplest to summarize them as follows:

- *Simple*: "Certain," decisions in real-time, based on simple true/false logic applied to simple cause-effect relationships with very high repeatability

- *Complicated*: "Certain," decisions either before or after the event, based on analysis of complicated but linear cause-effect relationships with high repeatability

- *Ambiguous*: "Uncertain," decisions either before or after the event, based on iterative experiments with non-linear cause-effect relationships that have only partial repeatability

- *Not-known*: "Uncertain," decisions in real-time, based on principles and values, in contexts with no discernible cause-effect relationships and low to no repeatability

The circular block in the middle is a kind of placeholder that, among other things, would be used for items that we haven't yet been able to sort into any of those four preceding categories.

The *five systems-theory principles* provide an essential checklist of patterns to watch for in enterprise-architectures:

- *Rotation*: A systematic process to assess a context from multiple yet related perspectives – such as a checklist or overview-diagram

- *Reciprocation*: Processes that create balance between systems or between components in a system

- *Resonance*: Positive-feedback or feedforward, which increase the "snowball effect" toward self-propagation, or negative-feedback or damping, which diminish the effect

- *Recursion*: Relationships or interactions which repeat or are "self-similar" at different scales – such as the classic hierarchical org-chart

- *Reflexion*: Holographic inverse of recursion – the whole is reflected in, and can be identified within, any part at any scale

Reflexion is perhaps the strangest aspect of systems-theory, yet one of the most valuable in enterprise-architecture. Through it we see that everything is connected to everything else, but is also *part of* everything else. A useful analogy here is a hologram: unlike an ordinary photograph, even the tiniest fragment of a true hologram will always contain a complete picture of the whole.

As shown in Figure 1-6, the five-elements model applies those principles of recursion and reflexion to any type of lifecycle in the enterprise:

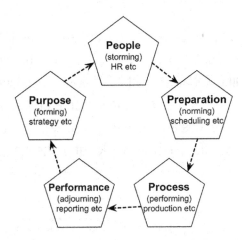

Figure 1-6. *Five-elements lifecycles model*

This is actually the same sequence as used in the classic Group Dynamics project-lifecycle – Forming, Storming, Norming, Performing, Adjourning – though here it is more generic, applying not just to projects but to relationships between different areas of the business, such as strategy, HR, scheduling, production, and reporting, respectively. The phases in the lifecycle also align well with key dimensions of *effectiveness*:

- *Purpose*: Focuses on *appropriateness* in the enterprise

- *People*: Addresses *elegance*, values, simplicity, ergonomics, and other human-factors in the enterprise

- *Planning*: Emphasizes *efficiency* – making the best use of the enterprise's available resources

- *Process*: Ensures *reliability* and availability of the functions and services required by the enterprise

- *Performance*: Assures overall *integration* between all the different elements of the enterprise

And the multi-dimensional segments-model provides a means to categorize anything we come across in our modeling of the enterprise. For compatibility, it draws in part from the classic row/column Zachman taxonomy that's well-known to most enterprise-architects, but has a number of significant differences. For example, this reframe adds a new dimension ("universals") as a separate row at the top, and also inserts an extra dimension of "asset-type" segments which categorize *types* of entities (Figure 1-7).

Note, though that, just as the action-cycle described earlier intentionally looks like much the TOGAF ADM, but is actually different, here the segments-model intentionally looks a bit like Zachman, but is likewise actually different. In both cases, the similarities are there to support some degree of backwards compatibility; but the differences are absolutely crucial, because they are what make it possible for our architectures to break out of the classic IT-centric box.

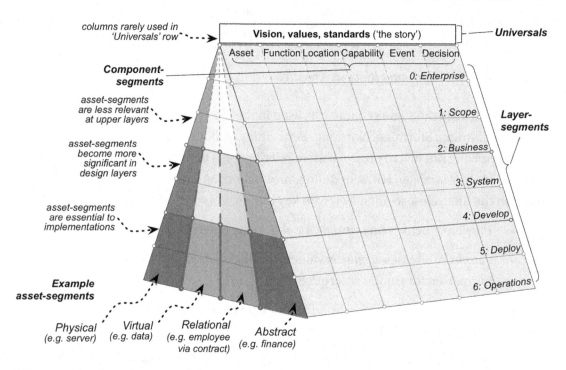

Figure 1-7. *Segments-model*

The "*Universals*" row represents a separate dimension, a kind of backplane to which *everything* must connect and align:

- **"*Universals*"**: Core constants for the overall shared-enterprise "story" such as vision, values, and standards to which everything should align – the key points of connection with enterprise partners and other stakeholders

Much as in the rows of the original Zachman framework, the *"Layer-segments"* represent types of responsibilities or viewpoints:

- *Row-0*: **"Enterprise"** – identifies the key elements of the enterprise as a whole, within which the organization will operate

- *Row-1*: **"Scope"** – adds possibility of change: key "items of interest" in each category, *without* relationships

- *Row-2*: **"Business"** – adds relationships and dependencies between entities: core entities described in business-terms

- *Row-3*: **"System"** – adds attributes to abstract "logical" entities, expanded out into *implementation-independent* designs

- *Row-4*: **"Develop"** – adds details for real-world "physical" *implementation-dependent* designs

- *Row-5*: **"Deploy"** – adds details of intended future deployment as actual software, actual business-processes, work-instructions, hardware, networks, etc.

- *Row-6*: **"Operations"** – adds details of actual usage: specific instances of entities, processes, etc., as created, modified, and acted on in real-time operations

Somewhat as in the columns of the original Zachman framework, the *"Component segments"* represent the abstract elements ("primitives") that we use to assemble a design.

Note that the terms used here represent actual elements rather than Zachman's abstract interrogatives, though the approximately-equivalent Zachman term is also shown in brackets (e.g., "What"):

- **Assets** ("What"): Physical objects, data, links to people, brands, finances, etc.

- **Functions** ("How"): Activities or services to create change, distinct from the agent (machine, software, person, etc.) that carries out that activity

- **Locations** ("Where"): Physical (geography, etc.), virtual (IP nodes, http addresses, etc.), relational (social networks, etc.), time

- *Capabilities,* often as *roles* or "actors" ("Who"): Human, machine, software application, etc., and either individual or collective

- *Events* ("When"): Physical, virtual, human, business-rule, time-based, or other event

- *Decisions* ("Why"): Reasons, constraints, and other tests which trigger or validate the respective condition, as in strategy, policy, business-requirements, business-rules, regulations, etc.

The *"Asset segments"* add an essential dimension that is largely absent from the Zachman framework:

- *Physical*: Tangible assets, mechanical processes and functions, physical or temporal locations, physical events; also Simple-domain *rule-based* capabilities and decisions

- *Virtual*: Intangible assets such as data, software processes and functions, logical locations, data-driven events; also Complicated-domain *analytic* capabilities and decisions

- *Relational*: Links to people (as indirect "asset"), manual processes and functions, social/relational locations, human events; also Ambiguous-domain *heuristic* capabilities and decisions

- *Aspirational*: Abstract assets such as principles, values, brands and belonging, morale and self-belief, locations within value-webs, some business-rule events; also Not-known domain *principle-based* capabilities and decisions

(There are also a few additional uncategorized segments such as for financial assets and functions, energy as an asset, and time as an event-trigger.)

These asset-segments represent what are actually distinct *dimensions* within context-space, and are fundamentally different from each other in scope and function. For example:

- *Physical assets* are "alienable" – if I give it to you, I no longer have it

- *Virtual assets* are "non-alienable" – if I give it to you, I also still have it

- *Relational assets* exist *between* two entities – if either party drops the relationship, it ceases to exist

- *Aspirational assets* represent relationships that are more a one-sided "to" rather than a balanced "between"

Most real-world entities we deal with in enterprise-architecture are *composites* that straddle across multiples of those segments. For example, a book is an asset that is both physical and virtual – object and information; a service is a merging of function and capability in which assets may be changed in accordance with decisions and events; and a business-model straddles every row, column, and segment of the entire frame.

Once we've identified the tools and techniques that we will use for the main cycle, we then need somewhere to store all of the information that's required:

Action: *Define and implement information-stores* or "repositories" for architectural information, including glossary/thesaurus, stores for models and project-management information, and registers for risks, opportunities, and other issues – see Appendix A.

That covers most of the "implementation" needed for this initial cycle. The project-diary for this stage includes some additional notes, most of which will carry over to the main cycle:

More random notes and jottings:
- architecture is often about the "non-functional," the qualitative
- is about development of judgement and awareness (otherwise all we have is "follow-the-rules," which destroys differentiation)
- use method and repositories to illustrate themselves
- OODA (observe, orient, decide, act) inside-loop in sensemaking
- serendipity, obliquity
- CSM: order = direct approach, unorder = oblique approach
- also CSM: in real-time we don't have time for analysis or experiment – everything that we do is the analysis or experiment
- decisions made in real-time may have impacts that last for decades
- dynamics of sensemaking – "go for a walk" through context-space
- content, context, connections, purpose

But as we noted in the previous stage, we'll also need some kind of concrete project-example, to ensure that we don't get lost in the abstract, solely discussing "the architecture of architecture." As shown in the project-diary, the example that came to mind here was a real client's enterprise-level concern about respect:

Real client business-problem as demonstrator

- loss of respect: "we've gone from the most-respected bank in our region to least-respected –
  what can we do about this?"

So we'll use this as a parallel worked-example throughout the main project-cycle.

Wrap-Up on Initial Cycle

Every architecture-cycle should end with a brief review. At first, we may seem not to have done much in this day's work, and it's quite likely there'll still be a lot of uncertainty about what we're aiming to do and what we'll achieve by the end of the overall project. But, in fact, we've now done most of the essential groundwork that will underpin all of the subsequent tasks – and as with all foundations, there's not much that will show on the surface! The value of that groundwork will become more evident as we move through the main architecture-cycle over the next few days.

Application

- How are architecture-projects set up in your own business context? What information do you receive with the work-request? What guidelines and metrics – if any – are defined so as to enable benefits-realization assessment on project completion?

- Do you work on your own, as part of a team of architects, or a more diverse team that includes people from a variety of organizational functions? If you work on your own, what options and actions do you have for peer-review? If you work as part of a team, how do you manage the group-dynamics and the respective roles and responsibilities?

- How do you identify the stakeholders for the project? The immediate clients for the project will usually be obvious, but which other stakeholders' interests need to be addressed, and how?

- What, for you, is the typical timescale and scope for an architecture project?

- What methods do you use to provide guidance and governance for each architecture project? In what ways do these methods change for different timescales and scopes?

- How do you start a project? What assessment takes place before you begin, and immediately after starting? How do you manage the inherent uncertainties at the start of each project?

- Which frameworks, tools, and techniques do you use in your work? How do you select these, and why? And do they differ from project to project?

- What information do you collect during architecture work? How do you store, manage, and maintain this information?

Summary

In this chapter, we explore what we'll need to get started on an enterprise-architecture project. We noted that this very first stage can sometimes feel challenging and disorienting, and that there's nothing wrong with that. We set up a basic sequence for the project. We then learned about the distinction organization and enterprise, and that in enterprise-architecture we create an architecture *for* an organization *about* the enterprise that provides its context. And for the implementation stage for this phase, we learned about four tools that we'll use throughout this project:

- Context-space mapping, used to guide sensemaking and decision-making

- Five key guiding-principles from systems-theory, providing a checklist of structural patterns

- A five-step lifecycle-model, describing a linked sequence of types of work within a project

- The segment-model, describing types and categories of content that apply in the development

We ended the chapter with an "Applications" section, providing a set of questions to help you to bring what you've learned here into your own work-context.

In the next chapter, we'll start the main architecture-cycle, with an emphasis identifying purpose, scope, and content for the architecture-project.

CHAPTER 2

Day 2: Purpose, Scope, and Context

At this point we start a new architecture-cycle, for which we've allocated eight of our ten available days: one day for each phase of that standard cycle that we set up back in Day 1. This will allow us to explore in more depth our "one idea" that things work better when they work together, on purpose. We summarized the basic structure and context of the architecture-cycle in the previous day's overview, but we now need to flesh out a bit more of the detail. Whilst working on this, we also need to make sure that each item links back in a fully traceable way to the business-strategy and suchlike

- *Phase A*: Define business-scope, business-purpose, terms-of-reference, and time-horizon(s) for the iteration; scope also identifies respective stakeholders and applicable governance for assessment and any probable implementation phases.

- *Phase B*: For the primary time-horizon ("as-is" or "to-be"), identify the baseline of what is already known in the architecture-repositories about the scope; then assess the context in more depth, adding content to the repositories as we do so.

- *Phase C*: Repeat Phase B for the one or more comparison time-horizons ("to-be," "as-is," or intermediates) specified in Phase A.

- *Phase D*: Do a gap-analysis for each "as-is" and "to-be" pair (from Phases B and C), to identify requirements, constraints, risks, opportunities, and suchlike for future change.

© Tom Graves 2023
T. Graves, *Everyday Enterprise Architecture*, https://doi.org/10.1007/978-1-4842-8904-4_2

- *Phase E*: Review the results of Phase D to allocate priorities to requirements and identify appropriate means to implement the requisite changes or "solutions."

- *Phase F*: Establish a detailed plan to handle the changes "from here to there" – in particular, dealing with the "people" and "preparation" aspects of change.

- *Phase G*: Architecture assists change-governance with compliance, consistency and inter-project synergies during implementation of the planned business change.

- *Phase H*: Return to architecture-governance to do a "lessons-learned" review in relation to the respective business context, and identify any needs for further related architecture work.

The task for *this* phase – Phase A – is to identify and document the key themes and decisions for the architecture-cycle. That's what this day will address. Much of this is administrative, setting the scope of the project and dealing with authorizations and paperwork – but we still need to think in architectural terms at all times.

Main Project: "The Architecture of Architecture"

There was a lot of effort that went into the previous day's setup-work, as the project-diary observes at this point:

Running a bit behind schedule – still playing catch-up to yesterday

---

But key ideas will often come up when we least expect them – and that's why the project-diary is so important, as a means to catch those ideas as they pass by. In this case it was a crucial cross-reference from William Beveridge's scientific classic *The Art of Scientific Investigation*:

from Beveridge intro:

"Elaborate apparatus plays an important part in the science of today, but I sometimes wonder if we are not inclined to forget that the most important instrument in research must always be the mind of [the researcher].

"It is true that much time and effort is devoted to training and equipping the scientist's mind, but little attention is paid to the technicalities of making the best use of it.

"There is [at present] no book which systematises the knowledge available on the practice and mental skills – the art – of scientific investigation."

In essence, this is the exact same concern that we're dealing with here in enterprise-architecture: "It is true that much time and effort is devoted to training the [architect's] mind," in terms of the available frameworks and methodologies and so on, "but little attention is paid to the technicalities of making the best use of it – the *art* of [architectural] investigation." That focus on "the technicalities of making the best use of the architect's mind" should probably become the central theme – the *parti* – of our main project here.

So let's get this iteration of the cycle started, doing it step by step:

Step 1: Identify Purpose and Scope of the Architecture Cycle

This purpose should always be described in *business* terms, and should *not* presuppose any particular solution, as another note in the project-diary confirms:

from peer-review meeting with Kevin S:

- don't start from "solutions!" – spend the time working on the problem-domain, the solutions needed will arise naturally from that

If we come across any ideas for solutions, they go into the project-diary for review later – but not for here, and not for now.

Here we do need to define what is and is not in scope for this specific effort. We should establish the breadth of coverage, the level of detail, the architecture domains, respective time-horizons for "as-is" and "to-be" of the enterprise for the cycle, and any existing assets, services, and capabilities that we're likely to re-use. And for a formal project we should record the results of this step in a first draft of a document called the "Statement of Architecture Work." For this less formal project, though, exploring the architecture of architecture itself, we can simplify everything right down:

- *Business-purpose*: Use architecture to explain and enhance the way we do architecture

- *Sponsor (primary stakeholder)*: Us

- *Breadth of coverage*: Mainly architecture itself, but also anywhere that architecture affects

- *Level of detail*: Anything we can usefully cover in the time available

- *Architecture domains*: It's mostly about architecture itself

- *Time-horizons*: as-is = now, to-be = ten days from now; to-be is first (to-be as primary, as-is as comparison)

- *Asset, capability, and services re-use*: Whatever architecture tools, techniques, and methods that we already have to hand

We don't need a formal Statement of Architecture Work for this – we can document it instead in the project-diary.

Step 2: Identify and Review Applicable Principles, Policies, etc.

These should be straightforward:

- *Policies*: Whatever we already have that applies to architecture in general in this work-environment

If they don't exist, that's something that we'll need to work on as we go through this main cycle. We place a note in the project-diary to document this, anyway.

Step 3: Identify Business Goals and Strategic Drivers

This is about where this item of work will fit within the broader picture of the enterprise. In a normal architecture-cycle we may need to do some chasing-around at this point to find out what they really are – because often the immediate client won't know, and may not even care. But for our purposes here, these again will be simple and straightforward:

- *Goals*: Enhance skills and capabilities of the architecture team

- *Drivers*: Enhance overall effectiveness of the enterprise

These go into the project-diary too.

Step 4: Establish Architecture-Framework Scope of Cycle

This uses the segments-model framework that we explored briefly in the previous day's work. In reality it's just a large checklist that we can use to do a first pass through the "problem-space," to give some initial suggestions about what is and is not in scope from an architectural perspective. Almost all real-world entities are made up of "composites" that straddle the framework's rather simplistic categories, and we do need to remember at all times that those entities *are* actually composites.

To guide our sensemaking and redesign, we need to end up with abstractions such as the "architectural primitives" of the framework. But we always *start* from the composites in the real world – all the things that we see, that we touch, with which we interact – and then run the usual design process backwards, from complete design back to their underlying components. Doing this will also help us to identify the models, capabilities, and suchlike that we'll need in the later phases, when we get deeper into architectural assessment.

That phrase "models, capabilities, and suchlike" is very much a shortcut here, of course: these are topics that can each fill a book just in themselves. We'll explore them briefly as we go through the book, but we won't have space to go into full detail on them here. For more on capabilities and capability-maps, see the book *Doing Enterprise Architecture*; for more on services and value-streams, see the books *The Service-Oriented Enterprise* and *Mapping The Enterprise*. You'll find more detail about each of those books in Appendix C.

In this case, we're not looking so much at the *outcomes* of architecture, but more at the skills and capabilities that are needed for architecture itself. From the framework perspective, this makes the main focus of the scope very simple:

- *Primary scope*: Layers row-3 ("system") to row-5 ("deploy"); capabilities to tackle all types of problems; implemented by people (via "relational assets")

We then work across the columns to assess what else might come into that scope:

- *Assets*: Quite a bit of information (virtual assets) and links to people (relational assets)

- *Functions*: It's more about capabilities, but we might need to consider how those capabilities link together with functions as architectural services

- *Locations*: Anywhere that architecture work takes place – physical, virtual, and/or relational

- *Capabilities*: Particularly the other capabilities needed for some of our support-services

- *Events*: Mainly relational "people-events," though others may come into scope as we move closer to real-time architecture

- *Decisions*: Many different types at every different layer – that's really what we're working on in architecture

As usual, all of these go into the project-diary for later reference, particularly during the architecture-assessment phases that are coming up next.

Step 5: Identify Other Stakeholders, Concerns, Requirements

The client or sponsor is the primary stakeholder – and, in this case, that's us. But we also need to identify anyone else who may be affected by the results of this item of architecture work, both within the organization and the broader enterprise. In essence, that's everyone, of course, but we can usefully split this into first- and second-order additional-stakeholders, in much the same way that we might partition a supply-chain from supplier's supplier through to customer's customer:

- *First-order*: Strategists; change-managers; project-leads; project- and program-managers; other architects; and system-integrators

- *Second-order*: Operations-staff (especially those doing front-line innovation); developers; other managers; other key players beyond the organization

It *is* important to remember that these might be anyone at all: for example, we may not often work with the organization's end-customers, but they are definitely stakeholders of the results of our work.

Later on, if we organize the architecture information-repository around the structure of the framework, we can link people and their responsibilities to each of the items that we've recorded in the repository. By defining scope in terms of the framework, as in the previous step, we also identify many of the probable stakeholders for architecture-work. We should also review the issues-register, risks-register, and our other architecture information-sources for other potential stakeholders whose concerns may be impacted by the project. It probably isn't all that important for this project, but for other more far-reaching projects, it can save a lot of heartache – and prevent a lot of angry calls from stakeholders who didn't appreciate being left out of the discussion...

We record all of this too in the project-diary.

Step 6: Identify Additional Requirements

For a larger project, there might be some additional organizational or enterprise-wide limits on time, schedule, resources, or the like. For this, probably the only real constraint is time:

- *Available time*: Ten working days

We add that item to the list in the project-diary.

Step 7: Finalize Plan and Secure Approval to Proceed

For a formal project, we would need here to add a lot more to the Statement of Architecture Work: define a plan of architecture activities that will address all the requirements, within the scope and constraints, conforming with the business and architecture principles, and so on. We would typically need to lay out the business-case and value-proposition for the project and its outcomes. We would also need to estimate the resources needed, and perhaps develop a roadmap and schedule for the proposed development. And we would need to document all of those items in the Statement of Architecture Work for the project, and present it for formal review, before asking for authority to proceed.

In this case, though, the plan is already set – we're simply going to walk through the architecture process to review architecture itself – and we don't need anyone else's authorization to do that:

- *Plan*: Use architecture to review architecture

- *Authorization*: Self

Once we've documented that in the project-diary, we would be ready to proceed to the first part of the assessment.

Example Project: "Respect," for a Bank

To illustrate each of the themes in the main project, we'll run another real-world project in parallel.

This example-project is actually a composite drawn from several real business-transformation assignments during the past few years. For obvious reasons of confidentiality and the like, many of the key details here have been changed, or combined from different organizations; but the issues and background described here are essentially equivalent to those in the originals.

We're contacted by the organizational-development manager of the largest banking group in this country, the regional arm of a global corporation. They have a problem, he says, and they want to know how enterprise-architecture would help. The project-diary summarizes that first meeting:

client-meeting (change-manager):

- key issue is respect: "we've gone from the most-respected bank in our region to the least-respected in just the past six months – what can we do about it?"

- consequences: loss of trust from government, active rejection in market, loss of market share

- short-term profits are okay – which keeps parent-group at bay for now – but can see profits collapsing in near future if nothing is done

- whole-of-organization scope but limited authority for change – will need CEO's full backing to make it work

- take-over of another bank last year – still working on integration

- feeling the effects of the then-current worldwide credit-crunch

- also says executives don't know how to do strategy, and have scrapped their strategy-team – is a key concern for client

It's urgent, he says, yet the organization is already struggling from "change-fatigue" arising from that take-over, and funds are very tight at present both from that and from the overall malaise of the banking sector worldwide. Their own enterprise-architecture unit only covers IT concerns, and is still at a fairly early maturity-level, so will not be able to do the work. He needs something that he can weave into his existing change-programs at minimal cost and with minimal disruption; he wants concrete suggestions on that from us within two weeks at most.

It's really important to note here that although there's no mention of IT in the client's preceding description, in the project-diary, the client's concern is still very much one that fits an enterprise-architecture approach, in that literal sense of "the architecture of the enterprise." This project provides another useful reminder that there's much more to enterprise-architecture than just IT.

Two key points came up in that meeting: these are clients who are able to think beyond just the short-term – which many organizations can't and don't – and they can see beyond surface symptoms to deeper causes. Both of those bode well for a true enterprise-scope architecture, which is clearly what this will need to be. What's not so good is that our client is the change-manager, but whatever we specify will need the CEO's full support – yet we're told he's a "numbers-man" whose main focus is the quarterly figures, so we may have a real problem right there.

This isn't a large-scale project, though, so we can run it with only minimal governance, using only a project-diary for documentation, rather than a formal Statement of Architecture Work. But we still need all of the details to define what this project will be, so we go through the standard project-start checklist:

Step 1: Identify Purpose and Scope of Architecture Cycle

We can derive most of this direct from the information we have so far, though one important question comes up in the project-diary:

---

which way round for assessment: as-is first, or to-be? – the to-be is actually more like an "as-was," about recreating the conditions of the past

---

The to-be is relatively easy to identify and describe, so we decide to do the as-is assessment first, because that's where the known problems are. The outcome of this project will almost certainly call for cultural changes, for which the usual guideline is that these typically take several years to embed: so we'll probably need to specify for intermediate time-horizons as well as for the final desired "future state."

Given that, we can now summarize the overall project:

- *Business-purpose*: Restore community/market respect that's been lost by the organization

- *Sponsor (primary stakeholder)*: Change-manager

- *Breadth of coverage*: High-level overview, organization-wide, extending outward into extended-enterprise (including community and government)

- *Level of detail*: Anything we can usefully cover in the time available, with an emphasis on the "respect" theme

- *Architecture domains*: Emphasis on business-architecture, but may extend downward into IT or other detail-level domains

- *Time-horizons*: to-be = three years from now, with probable intermediates at six months and one year

- *Asset re-use*: Internal documents, publicity material, external surveys, customer-satisfaction, and staff-satisfaction surveys

We document all of this in the project-diary.

Step 2: Identify and Review Applicable Principles, Policies, etc.

The banking industry is subject to many rules and regulations, with international, national, local, or organizational scope. However, most of those apply more at the detail-level rather than at the broader culture-oriented levels that we'll need to work with here, and the client makes it clear that those formal standards are firmly out of scope for us anyway for this part of his overall project. We're also working independently from the internal architecture-unit, so for *this* part of the work, the only governance-policies we'll need are our own:

- *Policies*: General architecture-governance

We'll need to identify applicable *implementation*-governance as we do the assessment, though. We note all of this in the project-diary.

Step 3: Identify Business Goals and Strategic Drivers

As outlined in that client-meeting, the initial goals and drivers are as follows:

- *Goals*: Enhanced respect of the bank – both from others and within itself – to at least the levels enjoyed a few years ago

- *Drivers*: Market credibility; government and community relations; medium- to long-term profitability

These go into the project-diary, together with a note that other goals and drivers may arise during the assessment.

Step 4: Establish Architecture-Framework Scope of Cycle

This may be quite difficult to describe, because clearly "respect" is an issue that pervades the entire organization and enterprise. When respect fails, it's usually because the organization has lost track of its business-purpose, which would take us right up to the "Universals" segments; but it's also about actual business-practices, all the way down to the framework's row-5 or row-6 layer-segments. We make this manageable, though, by remembering that we only need enough to build a quick "holograph" overview of the issues – not the classic "excruciating detail" about everything! The real emphasis needs to be on anything that affects the organization's links with people, both externally and internally:

- *Primary scope*: Universals plus layer-segments row-0 ("enterprise") to row-5 ("deploy"); relational assets (as links with real people)

Working across the columns will suggest other themes in scope:

- *Assets*: Mostly relational assets, also virtual assets (information)

- *Functions*: Any functions that change or impact on relational-assets

- *Locations*: Any location – physical, virtual, and/or relational – that impact on relational assets

- *Capabilities*: Any capabilities that impact on relational-assets

- *Events*: Mainly relational "people-events"

- *Decisions*: Any decisions, business-rules, etc., that impact on relational-assets

All of these go into the project-diary for reference during the architecture-assessment phases.

Step 5: Identify Other Stakeholders, Concerns, Requirements

The direct client here is the change-manager, who is an important stakeholder who'll be in charge of implementing any proposals that come out of this process. But within the organization, *the* key stakeholder is the CEO, because that's who holds the ultimate responsibility for the organization's "universals," and hence whose concerns and needs we most need to satisfy. Behind the CEO, of course, are the CEO's equivalents in the parent-corporation; and behind them the anonymous shareholders, whose benefit is nominally the highest priority for the corporation. Those who would be engaged in implementation of change would be viewed somewhat separately, giving us a stakeholder "stack" as follows:

- *Priority*: CEO, other C-suite executives and top-level managers, parent executive, shareholders

- *First-order*: Strategists; change-managers; project-leads; project- and program-managers; other architects; and system-integrators

- *Second-order*: Operations-staff (especially customer-facing staff); developers; other managers; other key players beyond the organization

Yet beyond all of those, as indicated in that earlier diagram of organization versus enterprise, are all the *indirect* stakeholders that the organization must engage with in order to create the desired "shareholder-value." Their respect – or lack of it – is our actual focus here, so we *must* include them in our list of stakeholders:

- *Indirect-stakeholders*: Clients, suppliers, prospects, non-clients, anti-clients, government, general community

This list of stakeholders goes into the respective section of the project-diary.

Step 6: Identify Additional Requirements

For this brief project, the key constraint is time – both our own, and those of the people with whom we'll need to engage. We will only be making recommendations, not doing implementations, so it'll be straightforward enough to identify funding- and resource-requirements up-front:

- *Schedule*: Ten working days (elapsed time)

- *Client staff-availability*: Key stakeholders (for information-gathering)

We add these items to the list in the project-diary.

Step 7: Finalize Plan and Secure Approval to Proceed

The client needs a written proposal that he can take to the CEO for approval: once that's signed off, we're ready to go:

- *Plan*: Review available materials; run two workshops (one for executive-team, one for representatives of customer-facing staff); derive strategy; deliver recommendations and proposals

- *Authorization*: Client (change-manager) for funding, CEO for authority to proceed

This completes the start-up summary documented in the project-diary.

Application

- How do you start up a new architecture-project? From where do you obtain information about the business-problem, the scope, stakeholders, applicable policies, and the like? How do you ensure that you have the requisite authority to do the work – especially if you have to cross silo-boundaries to do it? Who funds and authorizes the work?

- What frameworks and processes do you use to guide planning for architecture-projects? How do you estimate schedules, costs, resources-needs, and the like?

- When architecture-preparation highlights potential political issues – particularly concerns around authority or "turf" – what planning do you need to do to mitigate those risks?

Summary

Much of what we learned in this chapter was administrative: step-by-step, all of the detail needed to set up an enterprise-architecture project, identifying purpose, scope, stakeholders, and more. Every change starts from a business-question: we need to establish what that question is.

We actually did this twice: first for our main project, about using architecture to make sense of architecture; and then for the parallel example-project, a real-world business-critical issue that needed urgent action. Both of these projects we'll explore in more depth throughout the rest of the book. A key point in the latter project was a reminder that enterprise architecture tackles issues that are often much broader than just IT: in this case, a concern that was primarily about people, and that affected every aspect of the entire enterprise.

In the next chapter, we start to move into the practice, exploring how to find out what's going on in the respective context for the project.

CHAPTER 3

Day 3: What's Going On?

At this point, we begin the architectural assessment proper, to find out more about how "things work better when they work together" within architecture itself. We start with the "primary context" – the desired or actual context at the time-horizon we chose in the previous phase as the point to or from which we would construct our roadmap of "from here to there." Usually we would do the "to-be" assessment first, but in some cases – and our example-project is one of them – it's better to start with the "as-is."

Our other objectives for this phase are

- Select relevant architecture viewpoints that will enable us to demonstrate how the stakeholder concerns are addressed in the overall architecture.

- Select the relevant tools and techniques to be used in association with the selected viewpoints.

If we were to do this "by the book," the process-steps would be

- Check the project purpose with the overall business strategy, business architecture, etc.

- Develop baseline-architecture for primary context.

- Select reference-models, views, viewpoints, and notational standards.

- Create and update primary-context architecture models.

- Review primary-context architecture against qualitative criteria.

- Finalize building-blocks for the architectural scope.

- Conduct checkpoint-review for stakeholders.

© Tom Graves 2023
T. Graves, *Everyday Enterprise Architecture*, https://doi.org/10.1007/978-1-4842-8904-4_3

The reality, of course, is rarely as simple as that. In principle, those *are* the steps we need to follow; but in practice, it's almost never the neat straight-line sequence shown in those idealized process-diagrams, but something more like a ball of wool after the kitten has chased it across the floor a few times. We use the term "iterative" more as a euphemism than anything else: "chaotic mess" might be a more accurate term, given how it often feels...

In the early stages especially, the one thing we'll discover is that much, if not most, of what we've been told – or will be told – will turn out to be out-of-date, or incomplete, or just plain wrong. Seeming certainties often aren't. Every stakeholder has their own views, which each usually turn out to be only one side of a much more complex story: as Edward de Bono once put it, "everyone is always right, but no-one is ever right." And somehow, we have to make sense from all of this, and derive something out of it that others can *use*. But that *is* our task here: it's *our* responsibility.

The one most important danger is something we'd already noted in the project-diary:

Don't start from "solutions!" – focus instead on the problem-domain

---

Much of the time, though, that injunction against solutions is not quite right. We do *need* a real usable solution at some point: the danger is about *premature fixation* on any putative solution, rather than all solutions as such. In practice, we'll often need to create a temporary "solution" to give our stakeholders something to argue about and tell us that it's wrong – which it probably is, at first. But that "wrongness" then gives something else to test, iterating toward a solution that *does* do what our stakeholders need.

Yet the point here is that during most of this iterative process, we'll be "in the wrong" – and many of our stakeholders will be very quick to tell us so, too. Which is not pleasant – but that's what the work demands. In fact there's a very simple test here: *if it doesn't feel uncomfortable, we're probably not doing the job properly*. That's something to think about while we're working, anyway.

Main project: "To-Be" Assessment of Architecture

So: on to assessment for the main project, which we summarized in the project-diary as follows:

business-purpose: use architecture to enhance architecture practice
sponsor (primary stakeholder): us
breadth of coverage: architecture, plus anywhere architecture affects
level of detail: anything we can usefully cover in the time available
architecture domains: mainly architecture itself
time-horizons: to-be as primary, as-is as comparison
asset re-use: available architecture tools, techniques and methods

For this we'll be doing the "to-be" in this phase, and move back to the "as-is" – our current skillsets – in the subsequent phase. But how *do* we do this assessment? The project-diary records the sense of frustration and uncertainty here:

how do we use architecture to assess the architecture of architecture? feels like spinning in circles – no traction, no place to start…

The short answer is "follow the process": do it by the book, *but be ready to do something else at any time*, as long as it seems to make sense within the sense of the whole, then return to the structure of the process once that moment of certainty is lost.

Step 1: Develop Baseline Architecture for "To-Be" Context

Some architecture methods use the term "baseline" in a somewhat different way, but for our purposes here, the baseline is the description that we have for this architectural scope *prior to any assessment*. We create this baseline from whatever information that we *already* have about this context in our information-stores – models, requirements, the risks, opportunities, and issues registers, glossary and thesaurus, and so on. We defined the applicable items earlier in the project-diary:

primary scope: mainly layers row-3 ("system") to row-5 ("deploy"); capabilities to tackle all types of problems; implemented by people
assets: information and links with people
functions: how architecture skills and capabilities link into services
locations: may be physical, virtual, and/or relational
capabilities: architecture-capabilities and support-services
events: relational "people-events," others for real-time needs
decisions: many different types at every different layer

It's quite probable that, as yet, we don't have anything about architecture itself in the information-stores, because most people won't think of architecture as a subject for architecture. But if we do have any, we note that information, and perhaps build a small set of views and reference-models if it seems useful. In any case, we'll only need to do this once, as a known baseline to return to if we get lost during the various iterations of the assessment.

The baseline should always include any overarching enterprise-wide principles, standards, and the like from the framework's "Universals" segment, as identified during the previous phase. One example would be to summarize what architecture *is* and *does*:

- It's a *body of knowledge* about *structure, story, purpose, and value.*

- It's used in *decision-making* throughout the enterprise.

- It's used to guide *designs*, of any type, that would contribute in *practical and effective ways* toward the *aims* of the *organization* and *enterprise.*

We'll use that as an initial baseline.

Step 2: Select Reference-Models, Views, Viewpoints, and Notational Standards

Although there are plenty of frameworks and models already available for use *in* architecture, currently there are no standard reference-models for enterprise-architecture itself. The nearest that exist are the various certification schemes, which, at present, are suitable more for IT- or software-architectures than for a complete enterprise-wide scope. (The TOGAF specification does include a summary of skillsets for architecture, but again most of those are for IT-architectures only.) So if there are no standards, we'll make do with those we listed earlier:

- Five-domain context-space mapping

- Five systems-theory principles

- Five-elements lifecycle

- Four-dimension segment-model

That should give us enough to start with for now.

Step 3: Create and Update "To-Be" Architecture Models

Here we expand the baseline architecture into a comprehensive architecture for the iteration context – in other words, the architecture of architecture.

We won't do this in much detail here – just enough to get started, because the real changes will occur as we apply it in practice over the coming days, weeks, months, and years. What we look for *here* are ideas or themes that would describe our "architecture of architecture," and core *requirements* for that capability within the enterprise.

This aspect of assessment is mainly about *sensemaking*, and is also going to be iterative and somewhat chaotic – so, at the start, we deliberately *allow* it to be "chaotic," a free flow of ideas, and then allow some kind of structure to emerge from there.

Let's start with *context-space mapping*:

- Initially there is only Reality, "the deep unknown," before we've started any sensemaking.

- We begin sensemaking in the Not-known to collect new information, iterating back-and-forth between there and Ambiguous to identify usable patterns.

- We iterate between Ambiguous and Complicated to derive designs.

- We simplify designs – especially for software, or anything for real-time – by iterating between Complicated and Simple.

- **But** we never forget that the real world is actually Reality.

We could summarize this visually, as shown in Figure 3-1:

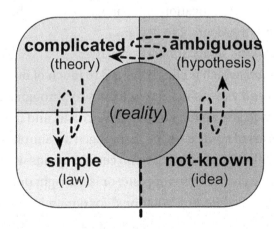

Figure 3-1. *Context-space mapping: iteration between domains*

This also clarifies the crucial distinction between architecture and design. They're actually flip sides of each other, but architecture faces toward the big-picture, the abstract, the overall aim or purpose, while design faces toward the detail, the concrete, the practical. On its own, architecture does almost nothing – it's only when it is literally "real-ized" through design that it becomes useful. Yet it's also where we're forced to be honest that everything we do is actually a subjective *choice* – whereas design can often pretend to be "objective," because by the time we reach the design stage, we're already following predefined rules. We could summarize this as in Figure 3-2:

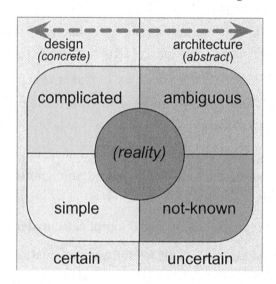

Figure 3-2. *Design and architecture: certain versus uncertain*

The outcome of this is that we need our practices to reflect where architecture sits within the overall functions of innovation and change: it's clear that it must have a large element of *sensemaking* as a precursor to design.

Next, compare against the *systems-theory principles*.

First of these is *rotation*, which is clearly central to much of our work: we rotate between multiple views and viewpoints, or work our way through checklists. We will want to use this both in any architecture that we create, and in the processes of architecture itself. In terms of context-space mapping, it's a Simple-domain technique: quick and easy, but with the risk that we have no certain means within the technique itself to assess whether the checklist is complete, or is the right one to use in that context. So while we will collect many different "rotations" for our architecture toolkit – another addition to our requirements-list – we would also need other techniques to select the *appropriate* ones for each context.

The architecture-development process is another "rotation," in that it provides a step-by-step sequence to follow – though note that it, in effect, defines a *default* set of steps, rather than the sequence that we would actually follow in practice. So again, other techniques would be needed to decide when to deviate from the default path, and when to return to it.

The next systems-theory principles are *reciprocation* and *resonance*, which, in practice, act as a matched pair, mainly in the Complicated domain. These will form a much-valued part of the architectural assessment toolkit, particularly to model dependencies, feedback-loops, and delays to optimize balance and effectiveness across the enterprise. But they may not apply that much *within* architecture itself: it might be useful to model some of the loops and delays in the architecture process, but that's probably all that we would do.

The final pair of systems-theory principles, *recursion* and *reflexion*, are fundamentally important to architecture itself – perhaps a key part of what distinguishes architecture from design. In terms of context-space mapping, they sit mainly in the Ambiguous domain, though also spread to other domains from there – for example, one of the key benefits of using recursion is that it can make designs a great deal simpler. The kind of architecture approach we're using here is itself highly recursive, applying the same basic principles in every part and at every level of the context and enterprise, while the architectural notion of the unifying *parti* represents a highly desirable example of reflexion.

Next, compare against the *five-elements lifecycle map*. Architecture itself is primarily focussed on the dynamic relationships between structure and purpose, which tells us straightaway that there'll be an emphasis on the Purpose and Preparation phases of the lifecycle. This in turn indicates the need for a great deal of attention on the People phase that acts as the bridge between them – which is what we see in architecture practice, of course, as shown in Figure 3-3.

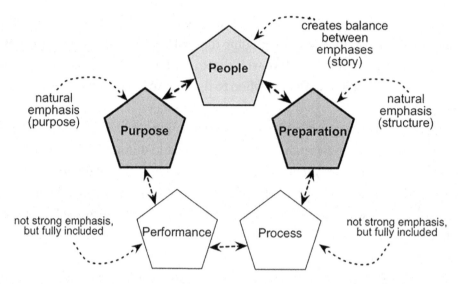

Figure 3-3. *Architecture emphases in lifecycle*

Architecture has its own Process activities, though it's not much involved in those of others elsewhere in the enterprise; but there would need to be significant attention paid to "bottom-up" themes coming *from* the production contexts, and also to metrics and the like both for and from the Performance phase. Note too that this five-element lifecycle is also an important example of architectural recursion – the same elements repeat at every level and in every context.

Finally, the segments-model *framework*. Back in Step 1 we noted the respective scope from the project-diary – mainly about *people* and *capabilities*, though we also need to look closely at *information* (virtual assets), at people-based *events* and, especially, motivation and *decisions* in general. These emphases are shown as the darker-colors in the segments-model diagram here (Figure 3-4).

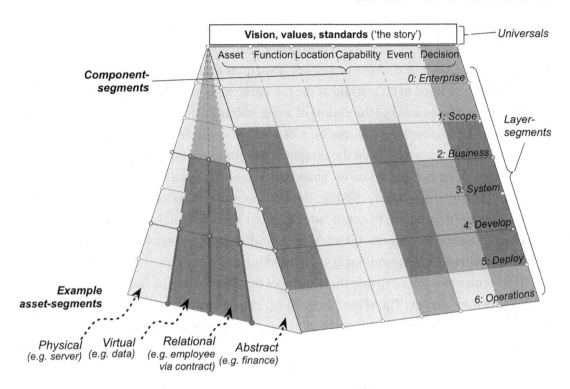

Figure 3-4. *Architecture emphases in segments-model*

For the *capabilities* or skills that we need in the architects (linked to the organization via *relational assets*), the project-diary notes a list from an article by enterprise-architect Sally Bean:

Sally Bean: "The elusive enterprise architect" (skillsets for architects):
- communicator and change-agent
- visual system-thinker and modeler with foresight
- fast learner
- principled pragmatist
- incisive consultant and troubleshooter
- "big picture" thinker

Architects also need to be consummate generalists, because they need to be able to link together every possible aspect of the enterprise, talk with anyone, and communicate meaningfully with the specialists in each area. (Soft-skills and EQ will often be even more important here than hard-skills and IQ.) The architects will usually need knowledge in breadth rather than depth – the respective specialists will handle most of the latter, although most enterprise-architects will also come from a specialist domain themselves. But even though the architect's depth of knowledge in any one skill may be quite low – sometimes just a basic understanding of key principles and technical terms – the sheer *range* of skills that need to be learned at the full enterprise-level scope may take literally decades to acquire: so despite the claims of some training-providers, true competency in architecture is *not* something that can be picked up in a simple one-week workshop!

On *assets*, we've already listed the tangible *information* used in architecture: items such as glossary and thesaurus, governance-records, risks and opportunities, requirements, and many, many models. But in some ways, what's even more important is the *intangible* information (a composite of virtual and relational asset, in framework terms): all those conversations and workshops and whiteboard-sessions that are so central to stakeholder-engagement and architecture practice.

Architecture *functions* provide the interfaces through which the items affected by architecture may change. Those items would typically be information and, especially, decisions, because architecture is primarily about decision-support. The overall functions would probably be much the same in any architecture context, but the architecture *services* – and hence the effective scope of architecture – will depend on the capabilities that can be plugged into those functions. As an entry in this morning's project-diary notes:

---

in essence architecture comes down to a single idea: things work better when they work together – role of architecture's is to ensure that things work better together over all of the respective scope (in principle, scope for enterprise-architecture is entire enterprise)

If the only available architecture *capabilities* and competences are in IT, then 'enterprise-architecture' will appear to be IT-specific, and so on. Yet, to extend our enterprise-architecture to the whole business and beyond, we don't need to change the architecture functions as such: we just need to extend the available capabilities – the range of skills experiences included within the architecture.

Architecture *locations* may be physical, virtual, or relational, but the latter are by far the most important of these – as in the old adage that "it's not *what* you know but *who* you know," and how and where to find those people. In the same way, we'll also need to know how and where to find the right information, the right decisions, and so on. But for architecture itself, we most need to know the decision-*makers* – which, in practice, comes down to real people, and hence the locations of those people.

The *events* for architecture itself, again, are mostly "people-events" – relational events. (There may also be a few time-based events such as regular scheduled reviews.) These connections may come in many forms – emails, task-requests, and many, many meetings – but the notion of an "event" that triggers a request for action is useful here.

In principle, the *decisions* assessed and acted on by architecture should again be able to cover the entire enterprise scope, at every level, from "universals" to real-time action and review. The architecture will need some explicit means to describe the purpose, role, dependencies, and jurisdictions of any or every decision in scope – the domains of the base-frame (Simple, Complicated, Ambiguous, Not-known) being one such categorization we might use for this. We would also need mechanisms to enable us to create a complete audit-trail for any decision, all the way back to the core-"universals" for the enterprise.

For each of these entities in scope – assets, functions, locations, capabilities, events, decisions – we would need a complete, fully maintained RACI matrix (responsible, accountable, consulted, informed) of all related stakeholders. (That's an ideal to aim for, anyway, though it may be impossible to achieve in practice.) This would tell us who would be affected by any architectural issue, who we should engage as active stakeholders in any assessment or review, and what clashes are likely where responsibilities and accountabilities overlap.

Given the models we started with, this would complete the first pass of the assessment. It might well be useful to loop back to the start and quickly scan through again to see if any other themes or ideas come up. In any case, we should document the results in the project-diary.

Step 4: Review "To-Be" Architecture Against Qualitative Criteria

The usual suggestion for this is that the core qualitative concern for capabilities is performance-management. Yet in practice, that's only *one* of the concerns here: we also need to add "universals" such as security, health and safety, business ethics, knowledge management, and the like.

For each of these, we need to identify appropriate *critical success factors* (CSFs) and metrics for *key performance-indicators* (KPIs). Which is not going to be easy, because the whole point of architecture is that it's about linking everything together – hence, in principle at least, its success can only be measured in terms of the whole.

Many of these metrics and suchlike will depend on the industry and enterprise, so I won't attempt to list them here; but the final lists should be documented in the project-diary, as usual.

Step 5: Finalize Building-Blocks for Architectural Scope

This is a step that we will probably have to skip over here, because it's not practicable in this context.

The "by the book" notion of Architectural Building Blocks and Solution Building Blocks, as patterns for re-use, is very useful in most parts of architecture. But architecture itself depends almost entirely on people-based capabilities – otherwise known as "skills" – and the concept of "re-use" doesn't work in the same way with people as it does with software or machines or other physical "things." One important reason is that people embody skills in very different ways to those in which we build capabilities into machines or software; another is that most of the architect's skills are in the "uncertainty" domains, which are naturally not amenable to simple re-use. Either way, probably best for now to document it as "not applicable," and move on.

Step 6: Conduct Checkpoint-Review for Stakeholders

This again would be simpler than usual, because the primary stakeholders for this project are us. Perhaps the most important point would be to review the list of requirements to date, recorded in the project-diary as follows:

- suitable reference-models, standards, techniques for architecture
- central role of sensemaking; role of architecture vs. design
- checklists and other "rotations" for the assessment toolkit
- fluency in sensemaking to select checklists, views and "rotations"
- fluency in identifying recursion, reflexion, and similar patterns
- fluency in strategic assessment (Purpose phase)
- fluency in "soft-skills"/people-skills (People phase)
- fluency in analysis and modeling skills (Preparation phase)
- familiarity and practice with architecture methodology (Process)
- appropriate performance-metrics for architecture (Performance)
- assets: workspace, computer, whiteboard, etc. (physical); information-sources and information-stores (virtual); access to people (relational); executive support for architecture (aspirational)
- functions: processes for architecture, including governance, quality, process-improvement, engagement, and delivery
- locations: meeting-spaces (physical); strong social-networks across and beyond organization (relational)
- capabilities: generalist-level skills for all competencies across enterprise scope; specialist-level skills in architecture itself
- events: contexts and interface-specs for architecture-events
- decisions: categories for decision-types; facility for dependency/validation "audit-trails" for any decision (or other entity)
- RACI matrices associated with all architectural entities
- appropriate set of metrics (KPIs), etc., and success-factors

If necessary, we could loop back to the preceding step 3 to re-assess our architecture-models and the list of requirements we've derived from them.

Once we're comfortable with that, we're ready to move on to do the same kind of assessment with our current or "as-is" context for "the architecture of architecture." Before we do that, though, we need to do the first assessment for our example-project.

Example Project: "As-Is" Assessment for the Bank

What should we do to assess the organization's architecture of respect? That's the challenge here...

We have a pair of workshops planned for this day: one for the executive-team, the other for frontline workers. That'll be important, because those are likely to be our main information-sources for this project – there's not much else to be had. But let's at least start off doing it "by the book," and see what happens from there. We're using the "as-is" as the primary time-horizon, because the overall aim is to recreate in the future the respect that existed in the past but does not exist now – so the place where we need to focus most of our attention is on what's changed between past and present.

Step 1: Develop Baseline Architecture for "As-Is" Context

This is short and sweet – or not-sweet, rather, because as yet we have no information available from which to derive that baseline.

In principle, we could derive at least a partial baseline from publicly available documentation such as the organization's annual report, together with some quick interviews with relevant stakeholders. In this case, however, it would have taken several days to do it, which we didn't have available to us, and we didn't have the permission to do it anyway.

Step 2: Select Reference-Models, Views, Viewpoints, and Notational Standards

There are no standard models for "respect" as such, but a decision-modeling standard such as the Business Motivation Model could be useful here, especially if linked to higher-level models such as the "Vision Role Mission Goal" framework (see Figure 8-18). For consistency, we'll also make what use we can of those four main base-frameworks:

- Five-domain context-space mapping
- Five systems-theory principles
- Five-elements lifecycle
- Segments-model framework

Ideally, we would model for a wide range of viewpoints, both inside and outside the organization. Realistically, though, we'll have to make do with whatever viewpoints we can derive from that pair of workshops, together with any information we can glean from other sources about the views of "outsiders."

Step 3: Create and Update "As-Is" Architecture Models

The first stage of the assessment is the two workshops: we'll then develop suitable models from the results.

Workshop for Executive-Team

This is organized as a half-day offsite session for the executive and other senior staff. Just under thirty people in all, of whom barely a third arrive on time – the remainder drift in over the next half-hour or so, without apology. Many of them ignore the no-phones rule for the session – including the CEO, who seems to be up and down like a jack-rabbit following one phone-call after another. The CIO even keeps her laptop open throughout the session, pounding away on an endless stream of supposedly urgent emails.

We use the five-element model as a central focus for discussion (see Figure 3-5). It soon becomes clear that, like many business organizations, they're strong on Preparation and Process – planning and production – but not so strong on Performance – completions, follow-up, and strategic use of metrics – and frankly weak on the Purpose and People domains. The nearest equivalent to strategy, for example, seems to consist of receiving a list of quarterly financial targets from global headquarters and then hacking out a quick plan that might deliver the required results – which could hardly be called a strategy at all. And the "people" aspects of overall planning were no better: the CIO, for example, was visibly overloaded from the strain of trying to complete the integration of the former banks' IT-systems, but she was doing so without any real support from the rest of the business.

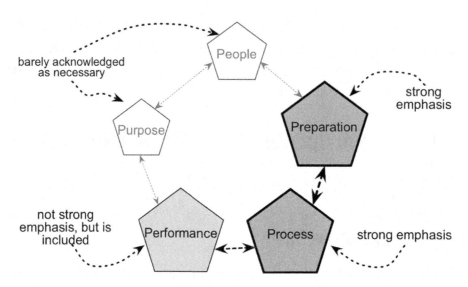

Figure 3-5. *Five-elements model for bank*

The theme of "respect" provides some interesting views into the overall context. While it's clear that professional respect between them is more than adequate, that's not reflected in their mutual *actions*: people talking over each other, others talking among themselves, while someone is supposedly presenting to the whole group, and, of course, the ubiquitous iPhones and excuse-me-I-just-have-to-take-this-call. There are a few displays of oversized egos, of course, but overall there's not as much political infighting as we've seen in other organizations, which ought to be a good sign – yet it seems extraordinarily difficult to get them to work together as a *team*. In that sense, respect *is* a serious problem here, right down to the way the senior management work with each other – or *don't* work with each other, more accurately.

What's not clear is what to do about all of this. But we shouldn't concern ourselves about that at this point anyway, because, as noted in the project-diary:

---

must exclude any consideration of "solutions" during the assessment phase – document any ideas and sketches, but don't discuss!

Instead, we simply take note of whatever information comes up, and hold back on any assessment until later.

Workshop for Operations Staff

This second workshop is a much larger affair, several hundred staff happily crammed into a local theater. For this we've joined with another team who have been running a more conventional organizational-development program involving music, group-work, and so on. It's also all in the local language, so we would otherwise only have been able to work through a translator – whereas here we're able to slip our questions into the overall mix, and note what comes up as a result.

There are staff here from almost every area of bank operations: tellers from main branches and in-store franchises, back-office staff, call-center workers, a few technical-support people. What becomes clear straight away, if masked by the laughter brought on by the skilled presenter, is that there are huge conflicts here, many of them caused by conflicting goals set by management for each group and business-unit. For example, one team's bonus is based on how much they cross-sell credit-cards to clients, while another team's is based on how much they *reduce* clients' over-credit. And *all* frontline staff – both customer-facing and call-center – are now bearing the brunt of customers' ire at the bank's response to the current worldwide "credit crunch," suddenly switching from an apparent policy of throwing credit-cards around like confetti, to endlessly haranguing every cardholder to pull back on their credit. At the executive level, the figures may look good, for now at least, but at the front-line *no-one* is happy... and that definitely does *not* augur well for the future.

Again, no "solutions" at present; yet it's noticeable that the simple fact of being *heard* seems to have made a real difference to the way these operations-folks now view their work.

Follow-On Assessment

We start with *context-space mapping*.

A quick summary, as shown in Figure 3-6, would suggest that – as is again common with many organizations – there's been an assumption somewhere that everything fits within the "ordered" domains, with little allowance for the reality of "unorder." Hence the too-Simple attempt to "take control," trying to force the market to change its behaviors to suit the organization's necessarily changed policies – and hence also an inevitable fallback to a market-context that has become "chaotic" in the wrong sense of the word. Much the same applies to the results of endlessly repeated cost-cutting within the organization itself: yes, it's "lean and mean," but there are now no reserves left to deal with the stress of change, and the strains are beginning to show, all the way up to the executive – not least in the CIO's increasing difficulties in keeping up with her insane workload.

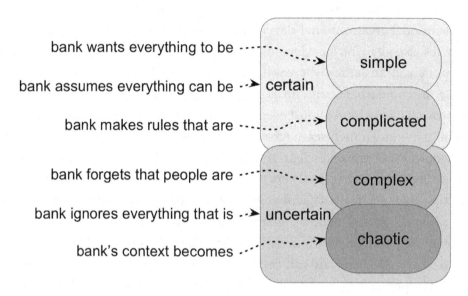

Figure 3-6. *Bank example: collapse from control to chaos*

Bank rules are usually structured for compliance and audit purposes. In principle they're not particularly complicated, of course – but they're often so vast, due to the nature of the controls, that they end up being experienced as complicated anyway.

Next, the *systems-theory principles*.

It's clear that both *recursion* and *reflexion* are in play here, because the overall respect-problems and stress-symptoms are all too evident throughout the organization and enterprise (recursion), and can be seen in almost any point within it and from outside it (reflexion).

There's evidence of failure to apply *rotation*, a consistent overview from every perspective – instead, each person seems to view the enterprise solely from their own standpoint, without much sense of the whole, or expressed feeling of belonging to a whole.

And there's also not much evidence of *reciprocation*, in that the organization seems to have a very one-sided, even self-centric view of its relationship with its market: in the CEO's eyes at least, "shareholder-value" comes first, with clients' needs a very distant second. The market-model suggests that this would lead to a very destructive *resonance* feedback-loop that would lead to spiralling damage to the bank's reputation – exactly as reported and as we've also seen for ourselves in those two workshops.

On to the *five-elements lifecycle* review.

This we can summarize direct from the executive workshop: the main emphasis is on Preparation and Process phases, with some on whole-system use of Performance, but nothing like enough of Purpose or People to provide much-needed balance. Seriously lopsided, in other words, if not unusually so for a commercial organization – but the longer-term impacts of that imbalance are now starting to show.

And finally, architectural entities in scope, in *segments-model* terms.

Almost all of this is about people, values, and feelings – or, in architectural terms, relational-assets (links with real people), "universals" (values), and the audit-trails of items and interactions (particularly feelings) that link them together. Architecturally, what's missing here is an explicit description of values to which everything can be anchored – the *vision*, or, as one of our other clients put it, "the totem-pole to unite the tribes." Just what that would be is far from clear at present: all that *is* clear is that "shareholder-value" isn't it, if only because that's of no interest to the bank's clients from whom that supposed "shareholder-value" would ultimately be derived.

In the project-diary, we also carried forward two notes from the previous phase:

- for phase B/C: will need to identify policies, rules, and regulations that would apply to detail-assessment and implementation
- for phase B (as-is): use POSIWID to assess implied-"purpose" of current systems

---

Policies, rules, and regulations may not apply until we start some kind of implementation – which may not happen in this case, and may not be our responsibility anyway. But we note an interesting clash of cultures: this country's culture places a strong emphasis on the family, the collective, whereas that of the parent-company builds everything around the individual – and most of the bank's metrics and bonus-structures reflect the values of the parent, not this place. That in itself might be a source of problems that need further exploration.

POSIWID is an acronym coined by the cyberneticist Stafford Beer, to describe the relationship between purpose and practice: "the purpose of a system is [expressed in] what it does." In effect, the bank is a "system" whose current effective purpose is to create the problems that we'd seen in that assessment. No one *designed* it to create those problems, of course – though "design" is actually a key source of the problems here, because these issues cannot be resolved by tackling them piecemeal, but only by tackling them as a whole, *as* a single unified system. That doesn't mean that we should try to do everything at once – that's impossibly disruptive, and it never works anyway. What it *does* mean is that we need to think architecturally, in terms of the architecture of the *enterprise*, not just the organization. And one key item that's most notable by its absence, perhaps, is the lack of any meaningful enterprise-scope vision – so that might well be a good place to start work.

But that's a "solution" – and all would-be solutions should be shelved until we get to the appropriate point, which is not here. For now, though, we've finished this part of the assessment: time to move on.

Step 4: Review "As-Is" Architecture Against Qualitative Criteria

To the CEO, it seems, almost the only thing that matters is the quarterly figures. But that won't work well enough in this context – not least because money won't buy respect. The whole focus of this exercise is qualitative, not quantitative – but it's still far from clear yet as to which qualities we'll need to focus on. Something we'd need to note in the project-diary, but otherwise just keep going.

Step 5: Finalize Building-Blocks for Architectural Scope

If we were to do this "by the book," we should look for re-usable building-blocks at this point. But once again that building-blocks concept doesn't quite make sense here, because almost all of this is about people rather than "things." Again, probably something best left to review in the next phase.

Step 6: Conduct Checkpoint-Review for Stakeholders

We finished all of the preceding review within about half an hour after the second workshop ended. Our client – the bank's change-manager – was still helping the main presenter to pack up at that point, so we're able to discuss the assessment so far. He's very pleased with what sees, so we get his go-ahead for the next phase – the "to-be" assessment.

Application

- How do you do architectural-assessment at present? What techniques, toolsets, and methods do you use?

- How do you avoid "premature fixation" on a solution during the assessment phase of architecture?

- How would you assess the architecture of architecture itself?

- If you're already doing enterprise-architecture, what domains of the enterprise does this architecture cover? How does it identify core elements such as capabilities value-streams and suchlike? If it does not describe all elements of the organization and key elements of the extended-enterprise, what assets, functions, locations, capabilities, events, and decisions would be needed for it to expand outward to cover that full scope? What are or would be the consequences to the organization if it does *not* fully cover that scope?

- How would you use architecture to tackle a big-picture business-issue such as "to enhance respect in the marketplace"? (Or – as in the case of a real business metric used by one of our government clients – "to increase the number of days between bad headlines in the newspaper"?) Where would you start? What planning and governance would you need for the assessment itself?

- What do you see if you apply POSIWID to your own organization's context and scope? If "the purpose of the system is what it does," what would you do, from an architectural perspective, to create change in that purpose, and why?

Summary

In this chapter, we explored the step-by-step process to derive an "as-is" or "to-be" perspective for the architecture. In the main project, we were able to do this in a straightforward way, following the steps as intended, in this case, for a desired-future "to-be" perspective. By contrast, the example project emphasized the "as-is" context, and also highlighted the types of challenges – particularly the people-related issues – that so often arise in real-world architecture when we're trying to capture the information we need about what's actually going on. The "Application" section at the end of the chapter showed how to apply all of this in your own work-context.

The main deliverables for the day were the respective assessments for either "as-is" or "to-be." The connections with people, and their engagement in the architecture, were also an important, if often under-recognized, deliverable.

In the next chapter, we'll see how to do the same kind of assessment to derive a "to-be" perspective for the architecture.

CHAPTER 4

Day 4: What Do We Want?

In this day's work, we do exactly the same kind of assessment as in the previous phase, exploring how "things work together," but this time, with the "comparison" time-horizon rather than the "primary" one. (We might need to do this more than once, if we need to assess architecture-requirements at various intermediate points.) So the fact that much of what happens here looks much the same as the previous phase is deliberate, and not a mistake. The whole point is that we need to ensure consistency throughout, hence the only thing that should change in scope is the time-horizon, from "as-is" to "to-be," or "to-be" to "as-is."

If we find that anything other than the time-horizon does change here – for example, exploring the comparison forces us to consider a wider scope in framework terms – it might be wise to review the results of the previous phase, and perhaps revisit that assessment to address the revised scope. It's essential that we can create a like-with-like comparison between these two phases, so that the gap-analysis in the next phase can make meaningful sense.

So the same key points from the previous phase also apply here:

- The steps shown are guidelines, not rules – expect to iterate back-and-forth, or even change the sequence.

- Watch for possible "solutions," but take care not to get attached.

- Expect to be viewed as "in the wrong!"

We do also need to be careful not to let ideas from the assessment we've just completed for the "primary" time-horizon to blur over into this part of the work: our gap-analysis takes place in the *next* phase, not this one.

© Tom Graves 2023
T. Graves, *Everyday Enterprise Architecture*, https://doi.org/10.1007/978-1-4842-8904-4_4

Main Project: Architecture "As-Is" Assessment

Once again we're likely to start with that same "don't know what to do" feeling of frustration and uncertainty. To help with this, a few scribbled notes that came up in the follow-on review from the previous phase were duly recorded in the project-diary:

---

architecture as-is, or "where are we now?" – probably no real baseline
most existing frameworks (TOGAF, FEAF, etc.) are IT-centric, perhaps moving slowly to business-centric: not enterprise, no standards, not much advice on what the discipline is
- "kind of get info together" – visuals, conversations, discipline?

The scope, obviously, is the same as before: anything to do with "the architecture of architecture" – particularly about the skills and capabilities that underpin the architecture disciplines.

As before, we'll start off by following the standard process "by the book," but expect to veer off somewhat as appropriate.

Step 1: Develop Baseline Architecture for "As-Is" Context

As with the "to-be" assessment, there probably won't be much of a baseline that we can create here. Existing enterprise-architecture frameworks such as TOGAF and FEAF are often very strong on models for architecture-content – particularly for IT – but are not so strong on *practices* or capabilities, which is the theme in scope for this assessment.

The TOGAF specification does include some useful sections on architecture skills and capabilities – particularly the chapters on Architecture Skills Framework and The Architecture Board. (The chapter-numbers may change between versions, but the chapters themselves are likely to be in each new version.) Note, though, that almost all of that material is still strongly skewed toward IT-architecture rather than enterprise-scope architecture: some "translation" may well be required for here.

For now, it's probably simplest to repeat the summary from the previous assessment, that architecture is:

- A body of knowledge about structure, story, purpose, and value throughout the organization and enterprise

- Used in decision-making throughout the organization and, potentially, the broader enterprise

- Used to guide designs that contribute toward the aims of the organization and enterprise

We'll take that as a working-definition of enterprise-architecture for this assessment.

Step 2: Select Reference-Models, Views, Viewpoints, and Notation-Standards

There's really nothing of this that should change between the to-be "then" and the as-is "now," so the base-models we use should be the same as in the previous phase:

- Context-space mapping

- Systems-theory principles

- Five-elements lifecycle

- Four-dimensions segments-model framework

Again, the main viewpoint that matters here is our own, but we'll need to be able to look at our "architecture of architecture" from many different directions.

Step 3: Create and Update "As-Is" Architecture Models

Much of the detail of this assessment will depend on your current architectural context and skills-base, but a quick scan with those same base-models – context-space mapping, systems-theory, five-elements, segments-model – will almost certainly show that there's nothing that's *fundamentally* different between "then" and "now." The difference will usually be in the detail: not the *type* of skill or capability, for example, but the *scope* that each would cover.

One point that comes up here is that we have almost everything we could want for our architecture – models, methods, frameworks, theory, tools, the lot – except for the one thing we need the most: what to *do* with it all. As we saw Beveridge describe earlier, the same problem occurs in other disciplines too: "It is true that much time and effort is devoted to training and equipping the scientist's mind, but little attention is paid to the technicalities of making the best use of it. There is [as yet] no book which systematises the knowledge available on the practice and mental skills – the art – of scientific investigation." Almost exactly the same could be said for architectural investigation: we have the "science," but not the "art" that makes it work.

Instead, it seems to be expected that we "just know" what to do – without any structure to that supposed process of "knowing." For example, as a colleague put it the other day:

It's like we kind of get information together till it sort of makes sense, then draw a picture, and then argue about it a bit, and then draw another picture, and take that to show it someone else, who tells us we've got it all wrong and it should be this way round instead, so we draw another picture, for another conversation, for another picture, for another conversation…

We're bringing together all these disparate views about the same thing – and people often don't realize that they're actually looking at the same thing.

The other key point is a problem about scope. Almost everything in current enterprise-architecture still revolves around IT: indeed, many practitioners would still believe that it is *only* about detail-level architectures for IT, and governance of IT-implementations. It's IT-centric in the sense that every conversation seems to end up being about IT, or IT-related aspects of a much broader problem such as security-architecture or knowledge-architecture or service-architecture. Although it is getting *somewhat* better these days, for a long time so-called "business-architecture" was little more than a kind of randomized grab-bag of "anything not-IT that might affect on IT." And much of that "business-architecture" was, and sometimes still is, so jumbled-up that almost no distinction would be made between business-strategy and run-time business-processes, even though they occupy very different slots even in the original Zachman framework, and represent what are *fundamentally* different viewpoints in the business-architecture. Even now, there's still often not much awareness of business *as* business, and even less of enterprise *as* enterprise. In that sense, it's questionable whether much of what purports to be "enterprise-architecture" is actually *enterprise*-architecture at all.

This mis-naming is also reflected in what's happening – or not happening – at present in the recruitment market. Even now it's still rare to come across a job-advert for an "enterprise-architect" that describes anything resembling a true enterprise-scope architecture role: almost all are actually describing IT-architecture roles, many of them very low-level indeed. Often the give-away clue is the job-title itself, such as "SAP Enterprise Architect", or "Java Enterprise Architect": a simple rule of thumb is that if there's a technology mentioned in the title, it ain't enterprise-architecture.

One way to resolve some of the arguments about what enterprise architecture is would be to ask what it isn't. We could do this by deconstructing that earlier description of the role of enterprise-architecture: that it's "a business-capability that manages a body of knowledge about enterprise structure, story, purpose and value."

It manages a body of knowledge, and it's also a decision-*support* system, not a *decision*-system. Decisions at this level are typically the role of strategy: in a smaller organization the architecture team may do that too, but it's not actually the core of the role.

- If it doesn't manage an explicit body of knowledge used in organization-wide decision-support, it's probably not enterprise architecture.

The core business role of architecture is to *advise*: "if you change the strategy, these are the implications on structure, this is the structure we will need; if you change the structure, these are the implications for strategy, these are the types of strategy that this structure can support," and so on.

- If it doesn't provide executive-level advice, it's probably not enterprise architecture.

It's about the overall enterprise – the ecosystem in which the organization operates, not just the organization itself (which is the preserve of business-architecture). If the scope is anything less than the whole enterprise – such as business-architecture or applications architecture or technology architecture – then it's a domain-architecture, not enterprise-architecture.

- If it doesn't have the ability or authority to tackle a whole-of-enterprise scope, it's probably not enterprise architecture.

It's a body of knowledge about structure *and* story *and* purpose *and* value, and the intersections between them. Hence, for example, if the work is only about structure, it's primarily an operational issue, or a straightforward structural issue such as software-architecture. If the work is only about story, without connection to anything else about structure or purpose, then it's probably just the high-level end of marketing. If the work is *only* about purpose, then it's actually part of strategy, without any actual attachment to the deeper reality of the enterprise or organization. In a small organization, an enterprise-architect may well also cover some aspects of strategy – such as IT-strategy – and will often cover aspects of operational structure – especially IT-structures – but the real role is about value *and* purpose *and* structure *and* story.

- If it doesn't deal with the intersection of structure, story, purpose, and value, it's probably not enterprise architecture.

All of these "not-enterprise" architectures are extremely important in their own right, of course. All of them are technically subsets or sub-domains of enterprise-architecture, and many of them will also have an enterprise-wide scope at times – which is where the "enterprise" misnomer came from in the first place. But the real danger is that if we call them "enterprise-architecture," it will often block awareness of the need for an architecture at a true *enterprise*-level – and that absence can cause *real* damage to an organization.

Step 4: Review "As-Is" Architecture Against Qualitative Criteria

This is essentially the same as in the previous phase: the same emphasis on performance-management and qualitative factors of the core-universals, and the CSFs and KPIs identified earlier. We need to do a quick check to see if there's anything else to add, but it's more likely that if there's any difference, it'll be because this "as-is" is a subset rather than a superset of the previous list.

Step 5: Finalize Building-Blocks for Architectural Scope

As in the previous phase, it's unlikely that the "building-blocks" concept will be of much use here: document it as "not applicable," and move on.

Step 6: Conduct Checkpoint-Review for Stakeholders

We'll only need to do a quick review here, because we're the only primary stakeholders for this project. The most important point is to review the list of requirements to date, as recorded in the project-diary:

- requirements, etc., essentially same as for phase B

other points noted:

- need emphasis on what and how to <u>do</u> architectural assessment
- potential dangers of IT-centrism, etc.
- need to ensure that domain-architectures (business, security, applications, capabilities, data, IT-infrastructure, etc.) are not mistaken for whole-of-enterprise architecture

---

As before, we might perhaps need to loop back to the preceding Step 3 to re-assess architecture-models and the like, and the requirements we've derived from them, until we're comfortable that this is a true picture of the as-is context. Once we've done that, we then need to move on to identify the gaps between "here" and "there."

Example Project: Bank Past/Future Assessment

In principle this should be our "to-be" assessment for the bank, but it's actually not that straightforward, as the project-diary explains:

---

respect existed in past, need to recreate it in future

What the bank wants as its future "to-be" is actually the same level of respect that it used to have in the past – or, perhaps more to the point, the *results* that were associated with that level of respect. So while we might describe this as a "to-be," what we *actually* need to assess here is more the real architecture of the past – as "as-was" – rather than solely an imagined architecture of the future. That makes this exercise somewhat different from the usual – but it's also that difference that makes it easier to see what's really going on during the creation of the architecture itself.

Hence another note in the project-diary, suggesting a probable tactic to use for this purpose:

challenge: "what does respect look like?" – use narrative, anecdote, etc.

After discussing this with our change-manager client, he gives us the go-ahead to hold another short exploratory session with some of the previous workshop participants. As usual, though, we start the assessment-process with the "by the book" sequence for this phase.

Step 1: Baseline Architecture for "Past/Future" Context

As before, there's really no information available to us from which to build a baseline: hence it's simplest just to skip over this for now.

Step 2: Select Reference-Models, Views, Viewpoints, and Notation-Standards

Here, we'll again use the same viewpoints and base-models as before: context-space mapping, systems-theory, five-elements, and segments-model, as described and illustrated back in Day 1. If some other frame comes up that makes sense in this context, we'll use it, though we need to take care that it will still support the like-for-like gap-analysis in the next phase.

Step 3: Create and Update "Past/Future" Architecture Models

The core information we'll need to collect is about what pertained in the past, and what's different between then and now.

Exploratory Session

The setup for this brief workshop is straightforward enough: a simple round-the-table narrative-circle session with staff from various levels and departments, to garner anecdotes around a few key questions:

- What did respect look like, or feel like, in the past?
- In what ways do you notice its absence now?

- Why was respect important to the bank?

- What else can you see that's changed between then and now?

- What suggestions would you have about how this can be improved?

Reviewing these anecdotes later, a few themes and examples seem to stand out:

– Relationships with clients:

  - We used to help people get what they wanted in life, now it feels like we're just trying to stop them getting what they want.

  - People think I'm only here to rip them off, you've no idea the hate I get down that phone-line.

  - The trust is gone – people don't trust us anymore, and we don't trust them.

  - It's not about service any more, it's about making money.

– Relationships within the bank:

  - We've got too big too fast – I don't know anyone any more.

  - There's just the two of us in our booth in the supermarket, I've no idea what's happening anywhere else in the bank.

  - Is there an "us"? I know we're supposed to be part of this big bank and all, but I don't feel it.

  - There still isn't a merger – we're still two separate banks, going our own separate ways.

  - I'm proud to be part of our team. I just wish I were proud of working for the bank – but the other banks here are worse, so what's the point?

– Relationships with the broader community:

  - I used to be proud to say I'm a bank-teller, now I have to hide what I do, pretend I've changed jobs.

  - Who would trust a bank these days? Do you? I don't – and I work here!

  - People think I'm one of the enemy for working here.

- We used to be the very first people the government would come to, to ask for advice, now we almost have to go in on bended knee before they'll listen to us at all.

- We spend a lot of money on social projects, and we always have, but no-one seems to hear about it – they don't know the good we do for business, for the community, for everyone.

– Changes in policy, and their effects:

- Reckon we've lost the plot somewhere – don't know where or how, but you can feel it everywhere.

- Something happened back at the parent company about five years ago – suddenly the only thing that mattered was shareholder-value. Must have been their bonuses or something, because all they wanted to hear from us was how much profit we'd made this quarter – they didn't care about anything else at all.

- They used to help us back at head-office, but they're just not interested in any of our problems any more – all they want to know about is the money we make for them. We used to feel like we were partners, now we're just servants, and they treat us like that, too.

- Up until a few years ago we did a lot of credit-checks before we let anyone have a card. Then it seemed like we had to give them to just about anyone, fast as we could, no questions asked, as long as they ran up a nice big credit-bill at high interest. People who were careful with their money were no use to us at all. But since the crunch hit, it's been panic-stations, running around like crazy to get the debt-level down, chasing customers every day to pay up right now on every scrap of back-interest, and of course they haven't got the money, no-one has. No wonder they hate us, really.

Some of these anecdotes could perhaps be dismissed as nostalgia for a "golden age" that may never have existed. Even so, it's clear that there's a definite sense of contrast between past and present, and also too much of a feeling of stress and isolation to be able to think clearly about the future. Architecturally, this is the information that we need most at this point.

Follow-On Assessment

One point that's important to note here: much of this part of the assessment is likely to be challenging for our executive-level clients, because it's the first time we *explicitly* demonstrate that there are real problems here that they need to address. It's essential, then, to keep our own opinions out of this as much as practicable: we're here as decision-*support*, not decision-*makers*, and the only people who have the responsibility and authority to make the kind of major decisions that will come out of this are the bank's executive.

We *do* have the responsibility to show what the problems are, and what their consequences would be for the bank, in a quiet, calm, dispassionate POSIWID sense. Whether we have the *authority* to do so is another question entirely, as we'll no doubt discover...

On to the assessment, then, first with *context-space mapping*.

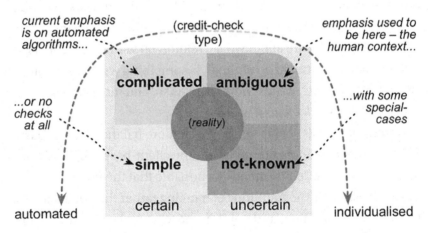

Figure 4-1. *Bank example: focus on human to keep things simple*

Figure 4-1 shows that, structurally, the main difference seems to be that the past was more centered in the more people-oriented Ambiguous-domain – less emphasis on control and calculation, more awareness of and adaptation to the real *human* context of banking.

We could go into a lot more depth than this, but that's probably all the time we have for it right now.

Next, the *systems-theory principles*.

The most obvious difference is in *reciprocation*: in the past, the relationships with all stakeholders were perceived as much more about mutual support. (Whether it actually *was* a relationship of mutual support is actually a moot point: what matters is that it was *perceived* as such. Where feelings are concerned, perception *is* reality – and it's feelings, and not necessarily facts, that are the glue that hold the enterprise together.) To use an ecological metaphor, the previous relationship was viewed by the bank's customers as symbiotic, whereas it's now perceived more as parasitic or predatory.

The key impact of this is on the *resonance* component for systems-theory. In practice, any business-relationship must include a reinforcing feedback-loop somewhere in its system, because that's what creates growth. The technical term is "positive feedback," which is a bit unfortunate, because "positive feedback" can actually be very destructive: what it grows is whatever's in the loop. In the past this loop reinforced that feeling of symbiosis; at the present time, the *same* loop is reinforcing that mutual negativity described in many of the anecdotes. We can't kill that loop, because it's an inherent part of the business-system: and even if we were able to kill it, doing so would kill the business, because there would no longer be anything to grow the business-relationships. What we *can* do is take more care about what's reinforced within the loop itself. But as to what that is, and what we should do about it, is something we leave for later phases in the architecture-cycle: for now, we just note that it is so, and move on.

The next item is the *five-elements lifecycle*.

From the descriptions, this seems to have been more balanced in the past: certainly a stronger emphasis on the People domain, with the client-base previously referred to as "customers" rather than "consumers." It's possible that the Purpose-domain of that time was driven more by the traditions of banking rather than explicit choices of policy – but that's only an opinion, and opinions have no real place in *this* part of the architecture-cycle.

Finally, review in terms of the *segments-model*.

At a conceptual level, the *structure* of the bank was essentially the same in both past and present. Key technology-driven changes in *capability*, such as the advent of ATMs, were already completed by the time of our "past" time-horizon; various upcoming changes such as Internet-banking and micro-payment via mobile phone still have a low market penetration here. The types of *assets* and *events* are much the same as in the "as-is" assessment; the range of *functions* and *locations* was partitioned somewhat differently in the pre-takeover state for the two separate banks, but the effective structural impact of those differences is quite minor. Most of the *decisions* column is much the same, too: the fundamental business-rules and regulations for banking in this region remain essentially unchanged.

The one place – structurally speaking – where there *is* a significant difference is in the "Universals" section, right up at the top of the framework. At this "past" time-horizon, there were two banks, not one, and each had their own distinct identity. And while profits and perceived "shareholder-value" were important, of course, they were not assigned the almost extreme priority that they have in the "as-is" time-horizon. Once again, though, we take care to avoid any opinion on this, but simply note the fact of the difference.

All of the information from the preceding assessments is noted and summarized in the project-diary.

Step 4: Review Architecture Against Qualitative Criteria

It's clear here that that the core of this is qualitative; beyond that, just about the only other point that's certain is that the current emphasis – placing quarterly-figures above everything else – was not there in the past, and is perhaps a key source of the present disjoint from the broader enterprise. The details of that, though, will have to wait until the upcoming gap-analysis.

Step 5: Finalize Building-Blocks for Architectural Scope

As before, the "building-blocks" concept doesn't really work here – though it's clear that the most important region of the extended-Zachman frame is the enterprise's "universals," and linkage to it from every activity and decision in the organization.

Step 6: Conduct Checkpoint-Review for Stakeholders

As before, the stakeholder-review here consists of a brief follow-up discussion with our change-manager client, summarizing the preceding results of the workshop. From this, we gain the go-ahead for a further meeting with him in two days' time, after the gap-analysis.

Application

- What do you do differently in your assessments for "as-is" and "to-be" contexts? How do you ensure that they stay separate, and are not accidentally blurred together? How do you ensure that you do not fall into doing gap-analysis in this phase, rather than keeping the focus solely on assessment?

- What for you is different between the way you do enterprise-architecture now, and the way you'd prefer to do it in future?

- How do you *do* your architectural assessment? What parts of it would you describe as the "art" or "craft" or "science" of architectural investigation? What processes do you go through? How would you describe these processes? How would you explain them to others?

- Assuming your work has an enterprise-wide scope, does it emphasize any one specific sub-domain within the overall architecture, such as business, security, applications, process, information, or infrastructure? If it does, who – if anyone – manages the architecture for all the other sub-domains? Who – if anyone – is responsible for linking them all together?

- If your work covers only a subset of the enterprise scope but is described as "enterprise-architecture," why is this? What implications and actual effects does this have for architectural integration across the whole organization and enterprise?

- How do you tackle assessment and presentation of highly charged "political" issues? What do you need to do to keep the stakeholders' focus on the architecture rather than the politics? How do you keep the facts – and feelings *as* facts – separate from the personal opinions and interpretations that drive the politics?

Summary

In this chapter, we revisited the processes of gathering the information for an assessment, but this time for the comparison time-horizon: from future back to the present, or from present toward the future. We emphasized that the methods need to be the same as before, to make comparison between the two assessments more meaningful. We also took care to *not* go into gap-analysis or "solutioneering": those tasks for later stages, not this one.

The example-project introduced us to the sometimes-fraught challenges of the "politics" of architecture, and why we need to take particular care around such issues. The "Application" section at the end of the chapter focused particularly on those themes.

The main deliverables for the day were, again, the respective assessments, for the comparison time-horizon for each of the two projects.

In the next chapter, we'll compare the two assessments via a gap-analysis, to derive requirements for change.

CHAPTER 5

Day 5: What's the Difference?

Now that we have architectural assessments for both the current "as-is" context and one or more probable "to-be" contexts in scope, we now need to establish the gaps between them, so as to identify requirements for change, and then document those requirements in whatever form we need for subsequent analysis and design. This is where we find out what's needed to make things work better by helping them work together, on purpose.

Note that this is only about *requirements* – not "solutions." Solutions are the way we implement requirements: they are *not* the requirements themselves. No doubt many ideas for solutions will present themselves during this period, but we still have to be *very* careful throughout this phase not to mistake a potential solution for any actual requirements. So whenever an apparent solution suggests itself – which will often happen here – our task is to note it on the project-diary, or the requirements-repository, or whatever else we're using to store that information, and then return straightaway to the quest for real requirements.

Another reason why this is so important is that the act of enquiry is itself sometimes the only "solution" that the context will require. All too often, I've seen IT people rush off to build or buy some complicated software system to "solve" some communication problem, when in fact the most practical, and cheapest, solution there would be the humble Post-It note – or just getting the relevant people around a table to talk for ten minutes. New technologies are like new toys – they're always fun for the first ten minutes or so. But once we've gotten over the glamor of the latest gadget, there's still the same work to do – and to make that work well, and be worthwhile, we need to keep the focus here on the *requirements*, and the effective gaps from which they arise.

© Tom Graves 2023
T. Graves, *Everyday Enterprise Architecture*, https://doi.org/10.1007/978-1-4842-8904-4_5

Architecturally speaking, there are an enormous number of places where gaps can arise: people-gaps, process-gaps, tools-gaps, data-gaps, information-gaps, metrics-gaps, finance-gaps, facilities-gaps, security-gaps, dependency-gaps, value-gaps, and meaning-gaps, to name just a few examples. (Some of these gaps may not be in our scope: if not, we still need to record them *somewhere* from where they can be retrieved later as required – such as for the baseline-architecture of a new architecture-cycle.) The point is that each gap implies requirements for change, and thence some kind of action to create the required conditions for that change.

The aim of the gap-analysis here is to identify services, functions, data-elements, capabilities, applications, and the like which may need to be developed, changed, or even eliminated entirely. We also need to assess the probable impacts of qualitative or "non-functional" criteria such as performance, cost, confidentiality, security, reliability and service-levels, and their whole-of-organization impact.

This applies especially to the many cases where one part of the architecture may need to change to cater for changes in another part of the overall architecture – and hence another reason why it's so important that the enterprise-architecture really *can* hold a true whole-of-enterprise view.

We need to do a gap-analysis between each pair of contexts – so if we have intermediate time-horizons between the main "as-is" and "to-be," we'll need to go through this process several times.

Most of this is straightforward: it's only about finding gaps, so it doesn't have anything like as much of the I'm-lost-I-don't-know-what-I'm-doing feel of the assessment phases. The only catch here is that the first couple of steps of the "by the book" version of the process are based on a "building-blocks" concept: we're supposed to construct and validate a matrix of the "as-is" and "to-be" architectures, and derive our change-requirements from that matrix. But while this works well for IT-systems and machines, it doesn't really work for people-based processes, skills, and capabilities. Despite the classic dreams (or delusions) of "scientific management," we can't partition real people into "building-blocks" in the same mechanistic way. So if – as is the case with both of our examples here – most of the architectural themes we're dealing with revolve around people, we have to tackle the gap-analysis in a different way. What I've used here is an architect's equivalent of the old "blink-comparison": place pairs of models on top of each other, and see what differences show up.

The main output from this will be a set of change-requirements, which we then use in the next phase to decide what actions to take and what – if any – "solutions" we need to develop, buy, build, or modify. We might need to create a model or two, and we're likely to identify additional out-of-scope requirements and issues: all of those should end up in a shared-repository, or at the very least should go into the final report for this cycle.

At the end of all this, we'll need to do another stakeholder review to confirm that we have the right requirements to go forward.

Main Project: Architecture Gaps

What we look for here are any gaps between what we already have in the architecture – the structure and purpose – of our existing enterprise-architecture, and what we'll need to embed in an architecture-of-architecture that can cover the entire enterprise scope. We'll need a special emphasis on tools and techniques that would help us in "the art of architectural investigation" – because those descriptions are what are most often missing from conventional frameworks and methods for enterprise-architecture.

Step 1: Compare "As-Is" to "To-Be" Architectures

Probably the simplest way to do this gap-analysis is to compare the "as-is" we identified in the previous phase against the following "to-be" checklists:

Scope

Every sub-domain would need to be able to reference any and all aspects of its enclosing enterprise, in the sense described earlier.

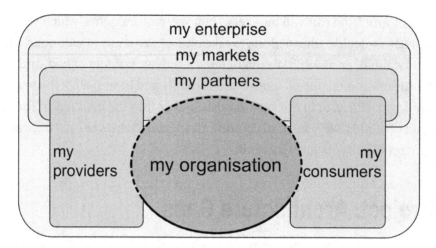

Figure 5-1. *Visual checklist for "enterprise" of a sub-domain*

A whole-of-enterprise architecture would need to be able to cover the complete scope of the enterprise: in other words, the literal interpretation of that diagram in Figure 5-1, with "my organization" representing the whole organization, and so on. For a sub-domain such as IT architecture, "my organization" would be the IT unit or the segment of IT within the respective sub-domain; "my providers" and "my clients" would be IT's own clients and providers; "my partners" would be the business-units and their business-needs that IT serves; and "my market" would be the overall business.

Within the sub-domain itself, we'll need to be able to distinguish between the abstract and the concrete, and we'll also need to be able to cover all aspects of the overall context. We could probably best summarize these via a simplified version of the segment-model, as shown in Figure 5-2.

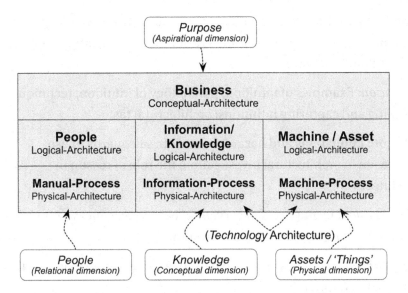

Figure 5-2. *Visual checklist for internal context of a sub-domain*

To do a gap-analysis here, we compare the "as-is" against each of those preceding visual checklists – and even for a sub-domain, we'll need to confirm that we *can* build an audit-trail all the way back to the key drivers for the overall enterprise. We identify any gaps, and then document them in the project-diary.

The Art of Architectural Investigation

The following summary, paraphrased somewhat from Beveridge's *The Art of Scientific Investigation*, provides a fairly complete checklist of themes that need to be addressed in architecture work:

- *Preparation*: Study; setting about the problem

- *Experimentation*: Architectural experiments; planning and assessing experiments; misleading experiments

- *Chance*: The role of chance in discoveries; recognizing chance opportunities; exploiting opportunities

- *Hypothesis*: Use of hypothesis in architecture; precautions in the use of hypothesis

- *Imagination*: Productive thinking; false trails; curiosity as an incentive to thinking; discussion as a stimulus to the mind; dangers of conditioned thinking

- *Intuition*: Examples of intuition; psychology of intuition; technique of seeking and capturing intuitions; architectural taste

- *Reason*: Limitations and hazards of reason; safeguards in use of reason in architectural investigation; the role of reason in architecture

- *Observation*: Examples of observation technique; general principles of observation; architectural observation

- *Difficulties*: Mental resistance to new ideas; opposition to innovation; errors of interpretation

- *Strategy*: Planning and organizing architectural investigation; different types of investigation; specific methods of investigation; tactics

- *Architecture and architects*: Attributes required in architects; incentives and rewards; the ethics of architecture; different types of architects; architecture as a way of life

We need to identify any of the preceding themes that are not already adequately covered in the existing methods and approaches for architecture. As in the preceding section, we should then document any identified gaps in the project-diary.

Tools and Skill-Sets

From the "to-be" assessment, the following would indicate the range of tools and skills that would be essential for a true whole-of-enterprise architecture – though we should note also the central role of sensemaking, and the key distinctions between architecture and design:

- Suitable reference-models, standards, techniques for architecture

- Checklists and other "rotations" for the assessment toolkit

- Fluency in sensemaking to select checklists, views, and "rotations"

- Fluency in identifying recursion, reflexion, and similar patterns

- Fluency in strategic assessment

- Fluency in "soft-skills" and people-skills

- Fluency in analysis and modeling skills

- Familiarity and practice with architecture methodology

- Appropriate performance-metrics for architecture

We need to identify any of the preceding items that are not already adequately covered in the existing architecture tools and skillsets. We'll document in the project-diary any gaps that are identified.

Architectural Entities for Architecture

During the "to-be" assessment, we noted a range of architectural entities, in the terms of the segments-model framework, that would typically be required within the architecture itself:

- *Assets*: Workspace, computer, whiteboard, etc.; information-sources and information–stores; access to people; executive support for architecture

- *Functions*: Processes for architecture, including governance, quality, process-improvement, engagement, and delivery

- *Locations*: Social-networks across and beyond the organization

- *Capabilities*: Generalist-level skills for all competencies across enterprise scope; specialist-level skills in architecture itself, such as modeling of value-streams

- *Events*: Contexts and interface-specs for architecture-events and triggers

- *Decisions*: Categories for decision-types; facility for dependency- and validation "audit-trails" for decisions, etc.

- RACI matrices associated with all architectural entities

- Appropriate set of metrics (KPIs), etc., and success-factors

We can use that too as a checklist against which to compare the "as-is," and document any gaps that arise from the comparison.

The end-result should give us a fairly detailed set of gaps that might need to be addressed to enhance our architecture-practice. It might also be useful to apply some quick priorities to this list, perhaps using the common MoSCoW categories:

- *M*ust have

- *S*hould have

- *C*ould have

- Can *W*ait until some later time

This prioritized list of gaps will then form the basis for everything else that follows.

Step 2: Derive Change-Requirements from Comparison

This should be straightforward:

- Given the gaps, what is it that needs to change, in order to achieve the required "to-be"?

- Given the required changes, what are the requirements to create those changes?

While doing this derivation, we may also note various constraints and other dependencies that may be relevant for solution-design and the like – for example, some changes may only be possible when others have already taken place.

Once this step is complete, we document the resultant requirements and constraints in the project-diary.

Step 3: Review Requirements Against Existing Dispensations

This step won't apply if we're doing this assessment for the first time, but may well be relevant if we're revisiting it at some future time. A "dispensation" is a record that some choice had to be made that went against the agreed rules of the architecture: a classic example in IT-architecture would be an essential software package that will only run on Unix, when the architectural guidelines assert that only Windows operating-systems should be used. In effect, each dispensation represents an item of architectural risk; so each time we revisit the same context, we should also check if any dispensations can be resolved. It's a governance discipline, nothing more than that, but it *is* useful as a means to monitor and mitigate long-term risk. That's what this check is for.

So here we should search the Dispensations register – if we have one – for any existing dispensations that cover or intersect with the context of this iteration – "the architecture of architecture." If we find any relevant dispensations, we should then review them against the "to-be" architecture, to identify potential requirements that could resolve those dispensations. In this case, those requirements would end up in the project-diary, as usual, though in a larger-scale exercise, they would be recorded in the respective registers and in the formal Statement of Architecture Work.

Step 4: Review Requirements Against Qualitative Criteria

This is where we check everything against the various qualitative criteria that we set up in Step 4 of the assessment phases. Back there we used those qualitative criteria to help us refine what we would need in the "to-be"; but here we're now dealing with *change-*requirements, which is a rather different game, hence some of the criteria may need to be different, too.

It's just another set of checklists, of course. Obvious examples we would need for this kind of review include costs, performance, volumes, and so on, though at times, we may need to be a bit more inventive in finding other criteria to test. For example, Zachman suggests specific criteria for each framework column:

- *Assets* ("What"): Inventory-management

- *Functions* ("How"): Yield-management

- *Locations* ("Where"): Capacity-management

- *Capabilities* ("Who"): Performance-management

- *Events* ("When"): Time-management

- *Decisions* ("Why"): State-of-change management

Given the IT-orientation of the original Zachman model, that set may be a bit incomplete for every type of scope and scale in whole-enterprise architecture, but it's still useful as an initial check. Of these, the one that comes immediately to mind is performance-management: we need our architecture responses to be *fast*, in the real hours or minutes or seconds of business-time – not merely dawdle along in the months or years of academic-time, as in the "Waterfall"-style architecture-cycles of some of the better-known enterprise-architecture frameworks.

We would also need to take note of those "universals" that apply to everything in the enterprise – criteria such as security, ethics, environment, health and safety, and so on. And we should also test each of our requirements against the performance-indicators and success-criteria defined for our own discipline, our business-unit and the organization as a whole.

For all architecture-projects, but perhaps especially for this "architecture of architecture," we should test all requirements against the "effectiveness" set:

- *Efficient*: Makes the optimum use of available resources

- *Reliable*: Can be relied upon to deliver the required results

- *Elegant*: Applies and enhances the human factors in the context

- *Appropriate*: Aligns with and supports the indicated purpose

- *Integrated*: Helps to link everything into the greater whole

The whole point of this review is to find out if any of our change-requirements need to be amended to align with those qualitative criteria. Any updated requirements should be documented in the project-diary, as usual.

Step 5: Conduct Checkpoint-Review for Stakeholders

Working "by the book," what we should do here is collate the results of all of the previous steps, then present these to the stakeholders for formal review under the governance procedures. But in this case, the main stakeholders are us, so this should again be straightforward.

What's not so straightforward is that while the "to-be" would be much the same for every architect, the "as-is" isn't: many architects will come from an IT-oriented background, while others may come from business-architecture, or process-architecture, or some other discipline entirely. In short, it'd be different for everyone. So, for the purposes of this illustration, we'll assume that the key change-requirement listed in the project-diary is as follows:

---

highest priority:

- enhance the process, speed and accuracy of sensemaking, especially in architecture-
assessment: needs to cover the whole enterprise scope and to link in with the "art of architectural
investigation" list

We'll then use that as a base for solution-requirements and choices in the next phase
of the architecture-cycle.

Example Project: Change-Requirements for the Bank

Here we aim to identify gaps between where the bank was a few years ago (the "as-was"
or "past" architecture) and where it is at present (the "as-is" architecture), so as to guide
choices about where they need to go in the future (the "to-be" architecture). But we do
need to be a bit cautious here: it's likely that even to *describe* some of these differences
could be politically explosive – to say the least – and we don't want to be the target in
the age-old game of "shoot the messenger." So we do need to be careful in how we frame
what we say here:

- These are the differences between the architectures.

- These are the implications of those differences.

- These are the change-requirements that would seem to arise from
  those implications.

- These are the types of choices, arising from those change-
  requirements, that would need to be made in order to move from
  "here" to "there."

- These requirements need to be reviewed, approved, and prioritized
  by the client.

- The final authority for all of those choices rests with the client – *not*
  the architect.

That's also why we do the stakeholder-review at the end of each of the assessment phases: it means that the client *has already agreed* that the two (or more) architecture-summaries are correct, hence all we're doing here is explaining the differences between them, and implications that arise from those differences. It *is* true that, by its nature, requirements-derivation is in part an interpretation, but we're not adding anything new to what they've already approved, and we're definitely *not* attempting to override their authority. For our own safety, we need to ensure that that point is clear to everyone before we move on.

Step 1: Compare "As-Is" to "Past/Future" Architectures

The simplest way to do this is via a "blink-comparison": place the two sets of models on top of each other and see what differences show up between them. The comparison for the "respect" theme highlights the following key differences:

- Change of fundamental policy by parent, from assisting clients with risk-management to maximizing short-term profit returned to parent

- Loss of clarity about collective identity, in part resulting from the takeover of the other regional bank

- Changes in relationships with clients, from risk-management, to near-abandonment of risk-management (especially in the general credit-card market), to increasingly strident attempts (often perceived as intrusive and bullying) to regain "control" rather than *management* of risk

One of the side-themes that comes up from this can be seen in the comparison of the two five-element lifecycle models shown in Figure 5-3. This indicates that the balance in the overall strategic *flow* of the organization – and in some ways even the flow itself – has been all but lost.

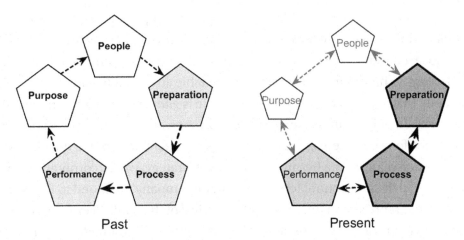

Figure 5-3. *Five-elements: balance in "past," imbalance in "as-is"*

The point here is that within the flow of the lifecycle, monetization occurs somewhere quite early on in the Performance phase. Yet monetization is actually an *outcome* of the overall lifecycle – and it's only available *because* the lifecycle is maintained in balance. But a common problem in commercial organizations is that all the attention is focussed on the monetization, to the extent that everything else may be regarded as overhead. As shown in Figure 5-4, the result is that the cycle gets short-circuited, instantly returning from Performance back to the start of Preparation – a role that middle-management would claim as their own – and leaving both Purpose and People out of the loop.

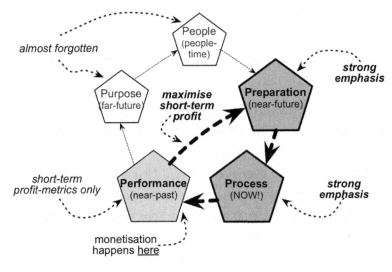

Figure 5-4. *Five-elements: the "quick profits" cycle*

This is actually the structure of classic "scientific management," and it does sort-of work, for a while at least... More dangerously, it will also seem more profitable for a while, because it doesn't have to carry the "overhead" of Purpose and People. Yet those two "unnecessary" phases in the cycle are what enable adaptability and resilience – and without them, that short-circuit version of the cycle is *guaranteed* to fail in the medium-to longer-term. To put it bluntly, any over-focus on short-term profit is now a proven death-sentence for a commercial organization: as Michael Porter put it, the obsession with shareholder-value is "the Bermuda Triangle of strategy, where corporations sink without trace." So in architectural terms, the parent-company's demand to focus on immediate profit represents a *huge* risk to the survival of the bank. Yet it's also clear that this is likely to be an "undiscussable," the elephant-in-the-room that no one dare mention. Perhaps all we can do here is to note the fact and its implications, and move on.

Step 2: Derive Change-Requirements from Comparison

Here we need to start with that list from the previous step:

- Change of fundamental policy by parent

- Loss of clarity about collective identity

- Disruptive changes in relationships with clients

And we then follow the "by the book" process:

- Given the gaps, what is it that needs to change, in order to achieve the required "to-be"?

- Given the required changes, what are the requirements to create those changes?

What the gap-analysis shows is that what most *needs* to change here is a shift away from the suicidal policy of the parent-company. But clearly, that's right up in the realm of the "undiscussables," and is not even within the CEO's remit here: there's nothing we can do about that in itself. But even so, we *should* list it as a requirement, because some option may come up during the solution-design process in the next phase. The constraint that we should record with that requirement is that we know we can't do anything about it *directly* – but that fact doesn't prevent us from finding some way to tackle it *indirectly*.

The other two items are more accessible: a requirement for some kind of metaphoric "totem-pole to link the tribes," and something to stabilize and improve the relationships with customers – both of which themes need to be described at first in *architectural* terms.

We document the results of this intermediate step in the project-diary, as usual.

Step 3: Review Requirements Against Existing Dispensations

This is very simple, because there aren't any dispensations in this context – or rather, if there are, we don't have access to them, so won't be able to take any into account. We note that fact in the project-diary, and move on.

Step 4: Review Requirements Against Qualitative Criteria

The simplest criteria to test against here are the "effectiveness" set: efficient, reliable, elegant, appropriate, integrated. We note that the key-theme for *this* specific architecture-cycle is "respect," hence we'll need to add a requirement that the human-factors strand of effectiveness – "elegant" – will need to be assigned a high priority when we assess our options for action in the "Solutions" phase. We also note that there's a real constraint of *time*: whatever we create as our "solution" in this cycle will have at most a mere couple of days in which to action something that will start to make a real difference.

These notes go into the project-diary too.

Step 5: Conduct Checkpoint-Review for Stakeholders

At this point, we should collate and summarize the key themes and requirements identified in this phase. For this context these would be as follows:

- minimize impact of short-term/profit-focussed policy of parent (constraint: direct change of policy is not possible)
- provide some means to anchor collective identity and unity
- provide some means to stabilize and enhance business relationships
- prioritize "human-factors" dimension in proposed solutions

Ordinarily, for such a politically sensitive context, we would set up a formal requirements-review, to move step-by-step through each part of the derivation, clarifying the reasoning at each stage. But in this case – partly from the client's own time-constraints, partly because this is a very quick consultancy-project anyway – the client has said that he'll skim through the list of requirements with us when we come to the "solutions" discussion on the following day. Nothing more to do until then.

Application

- How at present do you do gap-analysis between two architectures? How does this differ when the architectures relate primarily to "things" or IT, to when the architectures are primarily about people-issues and people-related themes?

- How do you link and test your gap-analysis to the organization's strategic and tactical goals, and its other "universals" such as vision, values, standards and suchlike?

- What processes do you go through to derive architectural and other implications from the respective architecture-gaps? How do you verify and validate those implications, and the processes used to derive them?

- How do you derive change-requirements from the implications? What kind of discipline do you apply to keep your own opinions in check while you do this interpretation?

- What processes, tools, and formal structures – if any – do you use to document, monitor, and manage the various requirements that arise in your architecture-work? With whom do you share those requirements, and how, and for what purpose?

- How do you derive and document politically sensitive requirements? How do you present them to your clients? What do you need to do to protect yourself against the classic "shoot the messenger" syndrome?

Summary

In this chapter, we explored how to do a gap-analysis between paired sets of assessments, and to derive change requirements from a gap-analysis. We again emphasized the importance of avoiding any jump straight into solutioneering at this stage. As before, the example-project also brought up "political" challenges for the architecture: we explored more about how to manage these. The "Application" section at the end provided us with a review about the process of gap-analysis.

The main deliverables from this day's work were the respective gap-analyses, and the sets of requirements derived from them.

In the next chapter, we'll use the derived requirements to start to map out potential solutions for each of the two project-contexts.

CHAPTER 6

Day 6: How Do We Get from Here to There?

Here at last we arrive at the "solutions" phase – the point where so many people seem to want to start...

As we've seen, the reason we *don't* rush into "solutions" straightaway is that, this way round, we're *more* likely to be able to address the actual problem at hand, and *less* likely to create the all-too-common kind of muddled, myopic, misaligned "solutions" whose inadequacies, assumptions, incompletenesses, and unintended consequences create more problems than they solve. Keeping "solutions" at bay until this point is a wiser way to go, really…

But this *is* now the time for solution-ideas – so if we've gathered any such ideas during the architecture-assessment phases, now is the time to bring them out and review them against the final requirements.

And this is also the point at which we turn away from the big-picture of architecture, and face toward the real-world detail of design – which needs a different set of processes, a different type of governance, often entirely different skillsets, and so on. Sometimes we'll be able to do this as part of our overall architecture-work, but it's more likely – and often more appropriate – that we'll hand over much of the detail-level decisions here to the respective specialists. We present and promote that architectural "one idea" that things work better when they work together – but these are the people who will actually make that idea real in the everyday business world.

© Tom Graves 2023
T. Graves, *Everyday Enterprise Architecture*, https://doi.org/10.1007/978-1-4842-8904-4_6

In effect, this is where we switch from decision-*making* for architecture, to decision-*support* for organizational change. And that will remain the core of our role and responsibilities in this cycle, all the way through the end of implementation, until we switch back to active architecture again in the wrap-up stage at the end of the cycle.

We've done all the architectural assessments; we've identified the architectural requirements and constraints. If we've done our job properly, that side of the work should be complete. Our objectives here are to provide *architectural* assistance while the client, the change-managers, and the like all identify, evaluate, prioritize, and select from among whatever options might satisfy those requirements, and assess the inevitable constraints and trade-offs for the various implementation choices. As part of that, we may also be asked to assist in identifying appropriate sequences of projects or staged "work-packages" to do the implementation – but again, our role here is usually that of decision-*support*, not decision-*making*.

The only other warning here is that *there may be no "solution" needed* – at least, not one that needs the full process and planning of a formal project or the like. We should *always* keep effectiveness in mind – efficient, reliable, elegant, appropriate, integrated – together with an emphasis on value. And also the age-old principle of "Keep It Simple": because often the best way to solve a problem is just to get the right people talking with each other at the right time.

Another useful example here is *kanban*, the "just in time" inventory-control mechanism at the core of the Toyota Production System. The word literally means "signboard" or "billboard," and usually consists of a simple card-rack in which physical cards each represent a signal that some component is required. Very simple, in fact almost *too* simple in many people's eyes: but in fact it works extremely well, usually far better than any IT-based alternative.

IT-development is expensive, of course, and ruggedized IT hardware suitable for use in an industrial context is even more expensive, but that's actually not the point here. Card-based *kanban* works because its very lack of sophistication means that there are fewer complications to break down; and the fact that the card is literally *tangible* does seem to help to support operations-folks' sense of what's actually happening on the production-line.

It does take real effort to find a truly simple solution to a problem: often a complicated "solution" will seem a whole lot easier, even though it won't be anything like as effective in the long run. And that's where the architect's eye for simplicity really pays off here, because the inexperienced specialist will go for "complicated" almost every time!

We don't expect to *deliver* any solutions here: all we should really be concerned about in this phase is to get our design-ideas right. The main outputs here will be some form of solution-designs, each described in fairly abstract, high-level terms; the detail of how those designs are actually implemented comes later. As architects, our main responsibility will be to ensure that any designs comply with the overall architecture, and with the requirements we found during the earlier architecture-assessments.

Main Project: Enhance "Architecture of Architecture"

At the end of the requirements-phase, we'd summarized our key requirements as follows:

---

enhance process, speed and accuracy of sensemaking in architecture-assessment, emphasizing "the art of architectural investigation"
must be able to cover whole-enterprise scope

We now need to decide what to *do* in order to improve the ways in which we do architecture – particularly the speed and accuracy of sensemaking – and to ensure that what we do is able to cover *any* required scope.

As with the other phases, it's probably simplest if we go "by the book" here, although at times we may need to deviate somewhat from that standard, and use other best-practices or patterns.

Step 1: Review Gap-Analysis and Change-Requirements

In the standard process, this is part of the handover from architecture governance to change-governance. In this case, we'll be doing any design and implementation within the architecture, so this isn't as important here as it is in, say, a large IT-infrastructure project. Even so, it'll still be useful to skip back and review the reasoning that brought us here, before we switch over fully into "design-mode, because those will form a key part of the inputs into the design-process." One particular point to note is the "audit-trails" from our requirements, all the way back to the core-universals for the enterprise, as recorded in our version of the segments-model frame: those trails will help ensure that whatever we do will keep "on purpose" in relation to the overall enterprise.

Step 2: Identify Business-Drivers and Constraints

In this case the respective "key drivers" were already described in our requirements: the need for improved speed, accuracy, and responsiveness, for greater overall performance for architecture.

Common business-constraints would include cost and availability of resources, but the most obvious constraint here is *time*. Most architects are overloaded with work, and we're unlikely to be any exception there: whatever we do here will need to be simple and quick, but it also has to be genuinely useful in our everyday work. That's a requirement that we'll need to carry forward in the design decisions.

Step 3: Derive Technical Requirements from Functions

The original version of this step was mainly about re-assessing IT-capabilities, centered around the "building-blocks" concept. Viewing the requirements in terms of functions, capabilities, and services would make it easier to identify what any system-implementation should *do*.

It's slightly different here because we're not deriving technical requirements: we're deriving *people*-requirements, centered around *skills*, which are constructed in ways that are very different from the simple mechanistic structures used in IT and machines. But a focus on function is still useful, because it describes what we need those skills to do, the kinds of changes that they should make in the context – which is what function *is*, in framework terms – and the interfaces and metrics that would apply when those functions and capabilities link together to deliver architecture-services. In that sense, the *functions* would typically include all of the activities within the architecture-cycle: analysis, assessment, sensemaking, decision-making, and the other items we derived from Beveridge's list as "the art of architectural investigation."

Those represent the *functional* requirements for this context; the "technical" requirements are the skillsets and skill-levels through which those services would be delivered.

The reality, of course, is that we're not going to be able to deliver against all of those "technical requirements," and in any case, many of those will already be in place – it varies from person to person. But one skills-component not well covered in most existing frameworks is sensemaking, especially at high speed: so that again seems a likely item to be worth exploring here.

Step 4: Derive Co-existence and Interoperability Requirements

Again, this step is primarily for IT, but it also has real applicability in other domains – or *across* domains, more often.

For our purposes here, the main requirement is that whatever we do with high-speed sensemaking for architecture, it would be best if it were compatible with sensemaking processes used in other domains and other contexts.

Step 5: Perform Architecture Re-assessment and Gap-Analysis

This step exists mostly for large-scale projects, where the items identified in the previous steps may well demand somewhat of a rethink about what we're aiming to do. For here, though, we're the only active stakeholders, so it's fairly straightforward: it's worth doing a final skim-through of what we've just done previously, but otherwise we're ready to look at our options for action.

Step 6: Develop Preliminary Solution-Designs

Our requirements for this are as follows:

- Enhance process, speed, and accuracy of sensemaking and decision-making in architecture, emphasizing "the art of architectural investigation"

- Must be able to cover whole-enterprise scope

- Must link back to the "core-universals" for architecture

- Be compatible with sensemaking in other domains

An obvious place to start would be a literature-search. For routine enterprise-architecture, this will show us quite quickly that there's almost nothing in the major frameworks about either sensemaking or speed, and in most cases, the scope is still arbitrarily constrained to or focused on IT, with little if any real reference outside of that domain. Some of the lesser-known frameworks, such as DyA and Pragmatic EA, do provide a stronger emphasis on speed, but their focus is often still more on IT than on anything else. Which is too limiting for our requirements: we'll need to look elsewhere.

A search with those requirements turns up two models that are not designed for architecture as such, but would otherwise seem to fit the bill:

- SCAN framework for sensemaking and decision-making

- "Observe/Orient/Decide/Act" (OODA) decision-cycle

SCAN is a very simple-looking frame – at its core, it's just a classic two-axis matrix – yet it's actually unusually powerful and versatile. The formal complexity-theory behind it probably won't be all that relevant for this purpose: the model's main value here would be to adapt its domains-frame as a *generic* base-frame for sensemaking. It's already used in that way in a wide variety of other contexts and business-domains, and could operate at any scale, from the detail-level right up to whole-of-enterprise. Its main focus, though, is on making sense of deep-uncertainty, especially for events that occur in real-time.

It's sort of the other way round for the OODA cycle: it doesn't provide any *framework*-support for sensemaking or decision-making, but it does place a very strong emphasis on speed: in fact its original purpose was as part of a training process for fighter-pilots, with cycle-times measured in seconds or less. As architects, it's unlikely we'd ever need to go to quite that level – though useful to know that the capability is there – but it certainly *is* useful to know that it can scale up or down to match any required timescale.

Neither of these models has everything we need, and neither is designed for use with architecture as such. But combining these two approaches with the existing architecture-cycle could give us what we need. So for now, we'll document that idea in the project-diary as the probable basis for our "solution."

Step 7: Identify Major Work-Packages or Projects

There won't be any "major work-packages" for this architecture-cycle: we don't have either the resources or the time. But if we use the classic categories of "buy, build or re-use," it's clear that it'll be a kind of combination of the latter two: we've already established that there's nothing we can use "off the shelf," but we can re-use ideas from SCAN, OODA, and the like as part of what we build.

Given the time remaining in this architecture-cycle, that means that our "work-package" for this purpose can take no longer than a couple of days to design and deliver – which means that we'll certainly need to keep it simple. We document those points in the project-diary, and keep moving.

Step 8: Conduct Stakeholder Review of Preliminary Solution Designs and Obtain Approval to Continue

We're the main stakeholders for this project, so all we'll need to do for this is to summarize our "project brief" from the notes in the project-diary:

---

link concepts from SCAN and OODA into the architecture-cycle

purpose is to enhance speed, sensemaking, and decision-making

to be usable straight away in real-world architecture practice

allow one day for design, one day for delivery, one day for review

---

That should be enough for now to define the basis for all of the remaining work in this architecture-cycle.

Example Project: Reclaim Respect for the Bank

We meet with our change-manager client at the bank to discuss what we've found so far, and what options he might have to start to address these issues. We can only have a half-hour meeting in which to cover the whole context, so we have to use a stripped-down version of the "by the book" method.

Step 1: Review Gap-Analysis and Change-Requirements

For this, we walk through the themes from the previous phase, as listed in the project-diary:

- Minimize impact of short-term-profit policy of parent.

- Provide some means to anchor collective identity and unity.

- Provide some means to stabilize and enhance relationships with clients and community.

- Prioritize "human-factors" dimension in proposed solutions.

At no surprise for anyone, our client immediately rules out any discussion of the parent company's policy: they're a fact of life, and we just have to accept it as it is.

We would have to admit that we did struggle there with one of the architect's occupational hazards: "the curse of over-responsibility." Clearly something *must* be done to change the parent-company's policy, because we can see that it's guaranteed to kill the entire organization in the longer term – but as "outsiders" it's literally none of our business, and we *do* have to respect that fact. There are real choices there – but they are *not* our choices to make.

Every good architect will have a great grasp of the big-picture, seeing all of the interdependencies and unintended consequences in that overview of the context. But the catch is that it's *only* an overview: down at the detail-level, things invariably turn out a lot messier than we might expect – especially when real people are involved, with all the tortuous, labyrinthine reasonings and relationships that that implies. Whether we like it or not, enterprise-architecture will always be entangled in enterprise politics: and as a colleague put it this morning, "if you're lousy at politics, you'll be lousy at implementation." That *is* a fact of business life, and we *do* just have to accept it as it is.

What we *can* do, though, and should do, is document what we see from that big-picture overview – in particular, the key implications and unintended-consequences that can't be seen down at the detail-level. And we need to make sure that those notes are available in a form that decision-makers *can* find and *can* use if and when they choose to look at the issue.

Beyond that, probably the only salve for our frustration is the Contractor's Creed: "ours not to reason why, ours but to do and charge…" Cynical, I know, but sometimes it does help…

But he does agree that if it's possible to design something that can mitigate the impact on the bank and its customers, but *without* questioning the policy itself, we should go for it. He also agrees with our assessment of the importance of the other two themes and the emphasis on human-factors. To him, he says, the "identity and unity" issue is probably the more urgent of the two themes to tackle, because that's the domain he deals with in his own work; but anything that would help on either of those themes would be valuable.

Step 2: Identify Business-Drivers and Constraints

The main constraints are time and cost: again, no surprises there. The most he can offer us is another half-day workshop for the executive, for which he can allocate a slot within a larger strategy-development meeting – though that's in just two days' time.

Steps 3, 4, and 5: *Not Applicable*

Given the time-constraints both in this meeting and for that future workshop, we'll skip over **Step 3**: *Derive technical requirements* and **Step 4**: *Co-existence and interoperability*. It shouldn't matter: neither of them are particularly relevant in this context anyway, because of the emphasis here on human-factors rather than solely technical concerns. In essence, we also covered **Step 5**: *Perform architecture re-assessment* in that part of the meeting, so we move straight on to ideas for potential solution-designs.

Step 6: Develop Preliminary Solution-Designs

Probably the only place where we can tackle the "respect"-problem – especially given the time-constraints – will be with the executive, and focussing on the whole-of-enterprise level. We flick rapidly through our "toolkit" of architectural themes and workshops, out of which two seem to stand out as our most likely options:

- Visioning

- Functional business model

Both of these aim to provide that much-needed "totem-pole to unify the tribes," but each will tackle a different part of the issues, and do so in different ways. The function-model is more about understanding what each person *does* within the organization and enterprise, while visioning is more about what each participant *is* – or chooses to be, rather – by identifying *the* key driver that links all the players together in and as "the enterprise." Just what that means in practice, and how to describe it, is what we'll explore in the next phase. For now we simply document that choice in the project-diary:

---

approved by client: executive-workshop will have two components: visioning exercise, and high-level functional business-model

---

Step 7: Identify Major Work-Packages or Projects

There are no "major work-packages" here: the whole package has to be completed in just two days, after all. What we'll need to do next – and fast – is identify exactly what we'll do in the executive workshop.

Step 8: Conduct Stakeholder Review of Preliminary Solution Designs and Obtain Approval to Continue

In this case, the "stakeholder review" is already happening in real-time, as we talk through all the different ideas and options with our client, the bank's change-manager.

This is a good example of an Agile-style approach to enterprise-architecture. In the conventional Waterfall approach, the architects will meet with the client only at discrete intervals, such as the formal stakeholder-reviews that mark the boundaries between phases of the architecture-cycle. But here, as in many of the variants of Agile software-development methodologies, *the client is an active participant in the design-process.*

This makes a crucial difference in several key ways. One is that, in working together, we have a better chance to arrive at a solution that will actually be of use: as an "insider," the client is likely to have a far better idea of what *really* goes on in the context than we "outsiders" could. But perhaps even more important is that the clients are likely to be much more tolerant of any difficulties that occur in implementation, because they've been actively engaged in exploring the myriad of tangled trade-offs that are needed in real-world design, and the inevitable kludges imposed by real-world constraints. Sorting out these issues up-front with the client may seem hard work at times, but it pre-empts what could otherwise be a lot of expensive arguments further down the track... and hence *definitely* worthwhile, for everyone.

The client signs-off on the preliminary decisions about content for the workshop, and – kind of important for us! – on approval for the respective budget spend.

And that's all we have time for in that meeting: the next time we meet will be at the strategy-workshop in two days' time. A lot of work to do to get ready in the meantime: we move straight on to the next phase of the work.

Application

- What processes do you go through to derive high-level solution-designs from architectural requirements? Which other stakeholders are involved in these processes, for which architectural contexts and domains? What governance applies to these processes?

- What are your main sources for information and ideas that can be used in solution-designs? Product-literature, journal-articles, white-papers, research-studies, and other material – what and where else do you explore? Do you look only inward to your own organization or discipline? Do you rely mainly on what the major vendors or consultancies currently have to offer? Do you look outside at other organizations or other business disciplines within your overall industry? Do you also look beyond, to other industries and contexts that have no direct connection to your own?

- How do you re-use and re-apply your architectural experiences and insights in the detail-work of solution-designs? In what ways can you re-use IT-architecture concepts, for example, in manual-process designs? Or offer-and-response practices from sales and marketing, perhaps, in designs for service-interfaces? How would you optimize this back-and-forth between architecture and design?

- How do you tackle contentious or politically sensitive issues with your clients? How do you manage your own feelings – particularly feelings of personal and professional responsibility – when clients fail to face, or even refuse to face, key issues that are creating real risks or actual damage for the organization? What discipline do you need to apply within yourself to *not* attempt to "take control" when others seem to be abandoning their responsibilities?

- To what extent do you use Agile-style approaches in your architecture, such as engaging your clients and other stakeholders as active participants in the design-process? What in your experience are the advantages and disadvantages of doing so? What impact does this have on your stakeholder-relationships? And what else could you do to improve your stakeholder-engagement?

Summary

In this chapter, we explored the first steps toward design, taking the requirements we derived from the gap-analysis, adding them to qualitative and other criteria, and then see what suggests itself as a possible solution. We then tested those preliminary ideas against the context, watching out for where "politics" and other issues might arise, and adjusting our plans accordingly. The "Application" section at the end of the chapter provided reminders and suggestions about how to tackle this in your own business-context.

The main deliverables from this day's work were the preliminary solution-designs, as approved by the key stakeholders.

In the next chapter, we'll flesh out those preliminary solution-designs into something that can be moved into actual implementation.

CHAPTER 7

Day 7: Step-by-Step Details

Now that we have the formal go-ahead to go and do something, we next need to plan out the fine detail of what we're going to *do* to make that "one idea" become real.

In a larger-scale program of work we would start by defining our objectives: sort through the solution-designs, develop our project-plans and delivery-schedules, cross-check all the intended-benefits and interdependencies, and finalize a migration-strategy and Implementation Plan (with proper capital-letters in the title). And all of this needs to be done under *program-governance*, or change-governance: in that kind of program of work, the role of the architecture-unit is definitely one of decision-support, not decision-making.

In terms of the five-elements model, by the way, this is mostly about the People and Preparation stages of the lifecycle: finding the right people with the right skills for the job, and developing plans for action. That action itself happens in the Process stage that follows, while the work that preceded this – the solutions-architecture phase – fulfils the Purpose stage for the lifecycle.

As you'll probably have noticed by now, architecture-assessment itself had its own lifecycle, of which the whole of this part of the work represents an outcome of its Process; both cycles join together again later in the final Performance stage. So in effect, what we've described as "the architecture-cycle" is actually *two* five-element lifecycles that intersect with each other, one focussed on architecture and the abstract, the other on design and the concrete world. Probably the key point here, though, is that there is explicit discipline and governance throughout the entirety of the cycle.

© Tom Graves 2023
T. Graves, *Everyday Enterprise Architecture*, https://doi.org/10.1007/978-1-4842-8904-4_7

In a smaller-scale architecture-cycle – such as that which we're running here – it's probable that architects would be more actively engaged in the design and delivery as well. But it is important to remember that although the roles of architect and of designer are closely related – are flipsides of each other, in effect – they are also distinct and separate, and subject to separate forms of governance, which is the point that needs to be noted here.

In this phase, it's also especially important to address any risks or issues that were identified earlier in the architecture-cycle, and also to take care to note any new ones that arise during this part of the work. Typical *architectural* activities here will often include advice on any inter-project conflicts and opportunities for shared facilities and other synergies – though again that would usually apply mainly in larger-scale projects or programs.

Because all of this should be under change-governance, the steps to be followed would depend on the project-methodology in use, and also on the architecture-domains and overall context. For example, the TOGAF standard suggests the following sequence:

- Step 1: Prioritize projects within the overall program

- Step 2: Estimate resource requirements and availability

- Step 3: Perform cost/benefit assessment of migration projects

- Step 4: Perform risk assessment

- Step 5: Generate timelined implementation roadmap

- Step 6: Document the migration-plan

- Step 7: Conduct stakeholder review of migration-plan

But again, that kind of structure might only be relevant in a large-scale transformation program: for anything smaller, we would usually aim to simplify it right down to the bare minimum that would still ensure appropriate governance, so as to minimize the performance-overhead of project-management.

We would usually expect to hold some kind of stakeholder-review at the end of this phase. But we might even dispense with that at times – especially for Agile-style development models, in which the equivalents of such reviews in effect are an inherent part of the overall process. We use whatever works, really – concentrate on effectiveness, but otherwise keep it as simple as we can.

Main Project: A Plan to Extend the Discipline

The simplest way to start off our planning here would be to revisit the "project brief" we derived during the previous phase:

- Link concepts from SCAN and OODA into architecture-cycle.

- Purpose: Enhance speed, sensemaking, and decision-making.

- Immediately usable in real-world architecture practice.

We've allocated just one day to do all of the preparation required for the "delivery" that will take place in the next phase. Which, perhaps unsurprisingly, exacerbates the usual uncertainties about any new and unknown item of work, as noted in the project-diary:

---

how to do this?? where do we start?? which aspects of architecture??
difficult to describe!! – hard to explain in words or in diagrams
need to get the balance right: "hard line" vs. "soft line"; verbal vs. visual; theory vs. practice; depth; recursion, reflexion, etc.

That note about "hard line" versus "soft-line" comes from the *101 Things About Architecture* book – "soft ideas, soft lines; hard ideas, hard lines" – which is actually about certainty versus uncertainty, rather than easy compared to difficult. Most IT-architecture deals with themes that are "hard" in the sense of *certain*, the hard-edged, rule-based distinction between true and not-true, in or out. Hence most diagrams in IT-architectures will be hard-edged, angular, abstract, boxes-and-lines. But the themes we deal with in "people-space" tend to be fuzzy, blurry, full of subtle uncertainties: so we perhaps need to express those qualities in the respective diagrams – such as via the immediacy of the kind of hand-drawn sketches that most architects would rough out on a whiteboard, rather than the perhaps over-polished Visio-style diagrams that would end up on a Powerpoint or in a book. These qualities are something that we'll also need to express in words as much as in diagrams, too. Something to think about, anyway.

As shown in Figure 7-1, the OODA loop is a cycle of action and response: observe, orient, decide, act. It's similar in some ways to the Deming or Shewhart PDCA process-improvement cycle – plan, do, check, act – except that the OODA cycle-time is *much* faster: often down to fractions of a second. At first it may not seem that that kind of speed has any relevance to architecture itself: but in some aspects of sensemaking in architectural assessment, we really *do* need to work that fast, riffling through vast swathes of ideas and alternatives in a matter of minutes at most. (As we saw right back at the start of this book, that emphasis on speed is what our customers said they want from us, at any rate.) Yet while it's often dismissed as "intuition" – if it's noticed at all – it is in fact a *learnable* skill: one that's extremely valuable to any architect. And the key to that skill lies in understanding the OODA loop, and linking it to architecture practice.

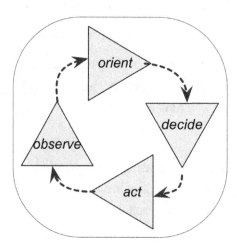

Figure 7-1. *Observe, orient, decide, act*

We haven't yet decided how we're going to present the respective material – a workshop, a training-session, a book, or whatever – but whatever we do, we're going to need to explain that loop, explaining the theory behind it but also showing how it works in practice.

We've also said that it would be useful to link this together with something like the SCAN framework (see the section on SCAN in Appendix B), as a consistent base to view *any* architectural context. Again, we would need to get the right balance between theory and practice: we'll need to show, for example, how to put it to use immediately on a live architecture project, and demonstrate that it really *does* help in sensemaking and decision-making.

But how would we express the *depth* and richness of this kind of sensemaking and decision-making in architecture? One option might be via those systems-theory principles, perhaps especially reflexion and recursion – such as through using those concepts to describe architecture itself. For example, we could perhaps link OODA and the SCAN-type domains together in some way, to form a kind of recursive "inner loop" within the standard phases of the regular architecture-cycle:

- **Observe**: What is "the context" here? And how do I observe myself observing?

- **Orient**: How do I make sense of what I'm seeing? And how do I make sense of how I'm sensemaking?

    - What parts of the context appear to be Simple, Complicated, Ambiguous or Not-known? Map out the "problem-space" in terms of those categories.

    - Given that categorization, what cross-maps would be useful for sensemaking?

    - Using the categorizations from the cross-maps, what available tools and techniques are "situated" in what regions of the maps' "solution-space"? What can I learn from this?

- **Decide**: Given what I have learned from sensemaking, what should be my "action-plan"? And how do I decide how I decide?

    - Select from the available tools/techniques.

    - Decide on a plan as to how, why, when, where, by whom, with what, and in what order each of the selected tools or techniques should be used.

- **Act**: What am I doing? And what am I doing as I am doing? – what do I see as I am doing?

    - Enact the desired action.

    - Apply the same overall OODA-loop to the action taken – recursively, where appropriate – for review, for further sensemaking, decision, and action.

- Repeat as appropriate.

It's perhaps important to emphasize here that the preceding is neither standard OODA nor standard SCAN. Instead, this needs to be understood simply as an illustration of the kind of thinking-processes that we go through in enterprise-architecture and the like, and the kind of context-dependent "mashups" from different ideas and frameworks and techniques that will arise from that work.

We can use that as a "hard" checklist – work through the sequence, tick off the boxes as we go – or as a "soft" guideline, giving an overall shape to what we would do, but without any hard-and-fast rules. Yet, to make it work, we would first need to explain the notion of "problem-space" versus "solution-space":

- *Problem-space*: The context in which whatever we're interested in is happening

- *Solution-space*: The space in which we decide what to do about what's happening

Ultimately, of course, there's only the context, "the real world": in systems-theory terms, the only accurate model of a system is the system itself. In that sense, both problem-space and solution-space are merely useful abstractions: they don't "exist" as such, nor are they actually separate or distinct. We create an imaginary separation between them so as to make sense and make decisions about what to do; and we "collapse" them together again at the moment we take action. What we might call "context-space mapping" is how we move around conceptually in those separated spaces:

- We work out what's going on – *Observe* in problem-space, *Orient* to link problem-space to solution-space

- We then select an appropriate way to respond – *Decide* in solution-space, then *Act* to link that abstract solution-space back into the real-world.

But all of this description is still too abstract: how do we apply it to the actual need, to deliver something that will help to "enhance speed, sensemaking and decision-making" within architecture?

The notion of "cross-maps" might help here: diagrams that link conceptually to other diagrams, providing different views into the same problem-space, or solution-space, or both, support the idea of "walking around" within that space to help make sense or make decisions. Examples might include different levels of repeatability compared to action-tactics, or to different types of decision-logic, or to cause/effect relationships; to quality-frameworks such as the Vision, Policy, Procedure, Work-Instruction model underlying ISO-9000, or the Plan, Do Check, Act (PDCA) cycle; to skill-levels, or to automatability; to timescales contrasted with levels of abstraction; to asset-types, or the layering of information and knowledge. These could also provide contextual "maps" where various types of tactics or tools or other "solutions" might align with specific types of problems, via cross-maps of respective characteristics and attributes. Something of that kind might help for decision-making here.

Start with a drawing, perhaps some combination of mind-map and SCAN-style domains in the star-diagram in Figure 7-2.

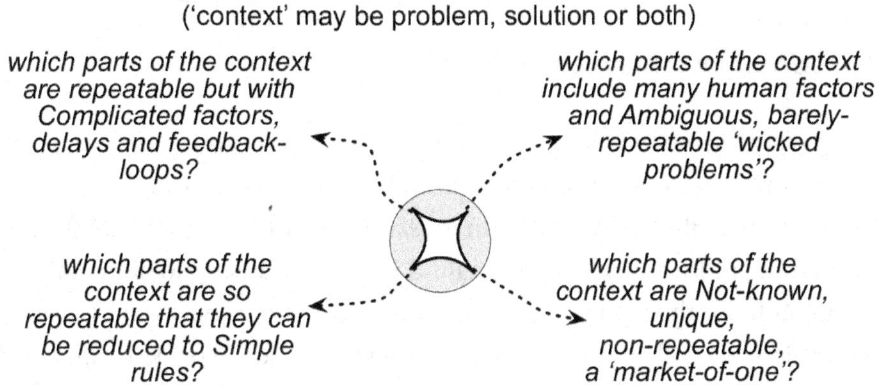

('context' may be problem, solution or both)

which parts of the context are repeatable but with Complicated factors, delays and feedback-loops?

which parts of the context include many human factors and Ambiguous, barely-repeatable 'wicked problems'?

which parts of the context are so repeatable that they can be reduced to Simple rules?

which parts of the context are Not-known, unique, non-repeatable, a 'market-of-one'?

Figure 7-2. *Describing the problem-space*

Doing that diagram highlights other detail-level requirements in problem-space, about the different type of skills and skill-levels that would need to be covered. Which leads to another cross-map in solution-space, about the applicability of different media to skills-development, as shown in Figure 7-3.

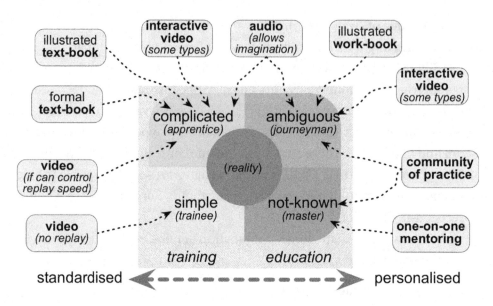

Figure 7-3. *Media for skills-development*

In-person would seem to be the nearest to an ideal choice, but it isn't an option that we would have here. Video is best for training, because of its immediacy and visual impact, but is also usually the worst option for *skills*-development, for exactly the same reasons; something more discursive, more fluid in its relationship to personal-time, would be a better fit for the actual requirements. So text and visuals would probably work well for this, especially if in a freer style – "soft lines," so to speak. Language that engages, speaking *with* rather than *to* or *at*, creating space for others to find their *own* architectural "voice," beyond all those by-the-book checklists. And "soft lines" in the form of hand-drawn sketches or the like, as a way to emphasize the speed at which architectural sensemaking and decision-making actually needs to take place – rather than the kind of polished "proper" diagrams which only arise *after* all the thinking-work is already complete.

We'll need examples to illustrate how this all works: recursively, perhaps the best example would be this process itself. In itself, that might be too abstract: we'll need to parallel that with another example, closer to the kind of architecture that actually happens within organizations – though it would be good to use an example that's *not* the usual mainstream of IT-architecture and the like, but shows how the same architectural principles apply in other business contexts. So perhaps something more about *values* than "things" – the *values-architecture* that underpins the organization's value-propositions to its client-base and its market.

Which, when we look back at what we've just done, is actually an appropriate plan for what we're aiming to deliver. We duly note this in the project-diary:

- introduce a new conceptual tool for architecture: "context-space mapping," linking the OODA decision-cycle and SCAN-like sensemaking into the standard architecture-cycle
- introduce it in the form of text and visuals, using a "soft lines" approach and style for both
- illustrate systems-principles concepts such as recursion by using the tool itself, and its usage, as its own example

---

And in effect, we can use the technique itself to sense and adapt what we're doing, while we're doing it, in the midst of explaining it – completely recursive, even able to change the architecture of the architecture itself in real-time. An interesting challenge...

So that's the project-plan: now we need to go ahead to implement it – which is what happens in the next phase.

But in the meantime, there's still further work to do on the real-life example: what *do* we do to start reclaiming respect for a bank?

Example Project: Envisioning Vision at the Bank

We start the planning-phase by reviewing the brief:

- Half-day workshop for senior-management and executive-level staff

- Develop the basis for a high-level enterprise-architecture, without using the word "architecture" (because most of these executives still think that architecture is only about IT)

- Ensure that it can be linked in to any other architecture and transformation activities already happening with the organization

- Two components authorized: visioning exercise, and high-level functional business-model

- Essential: *must* avoid anything that might be seen as politically sensitive, especially in terms of relations with the parent-company

And we have just one day in which to develop a complete plan for all of this.

Visioning Exercise

Visioning for enterprise-architecture *ought* to be straightforward, except that almost everyone gets it wrong. It's not a description of some preferred "future state" – which is how TOGAF presents it – or, worse, a piece of marketing puff – which is how the Business Motivation Model presents it. Instead, it should be a very simple single-phrase summary of what the enterprise *is* and what it *values* – and that therefore acts as a permanent "guiding star" for everything the organization does in relation to its enterprise-ecosystem.

For example, as described in ISO-9000 – one of the few standards that *does* "get" the real role and function of enterprise vision – the vision-statement acts as the ultimate anchor for the organization's quality-system; it provides the core-reference for all enterprise-relationships, for all internal relationships, and so on. And while it *is* also the core-reference for all marketing, it's *not* about some kind of "image" or short-term "market-positioning." In fact, if the vision ever does change, the organization is no longer in the same shared-enterprise, and even ceases to be the same organization – it's *that* fundamental to what the organization is and does.

More importantly, for this context, it forms an explicit statement about what the organization stands for, and the core reasons and relationships it will share with others. Hence it also defines the values against which the organization expects to be measured – which, in turn, form the source for mutual respect. So if the bank wants to tackle its problem of respect, it *must* have a vision that makes immediate and *practical* sense, to everyone involved.

The catch is that it usually takes people days to get started on this, and months to build – and we'll only have a couple of hours at most. But we do already have a standard framework for this kind of visioning-workshop: if we strip it back to a bare-bones version, we'll be able to do *something* useful in that time – we can be fairly sure of that. What matters now is how it links in with everything else.

Functional Business Model

What we describe as a "functional business model" is also known by a number of other names, such as "business overview model" or "business capability model." Often described as "the organization on a page," it presents a summary of all of the core functions or capabilities of the organization, usually in visual form. Although it will generally use some kind of hierarchical layout, with functions nested inside "parent" business-functions, it is *not* the same as the usual org-chart: it's about function, not management.

At the topmost layer ("tier-1"), almost every organization will look alike. There's a set of functions that cover strategy and planning; another that deals with customer-contacts and the like; another cluster that deals with "stuff" coming in, that do something to that stuff, and that deals with what has to happen to that stuff as it goes out again; and another that deals with all the follow-through after the stuff has been delivered. Underpinning all of that is a layer that includes all of the support-functions – HR, computing, logistics, facilities, finance, and so on. There are a few variations on that theme, but otherwise it's always much the same, as shown in Figure 7-4.

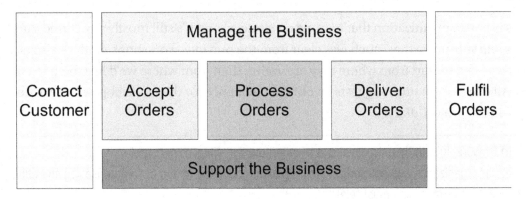

Figure 7-4. *Tier-1 of generic functional business model*

Organizations start to differentiate from each other as we go down into the next tier of functions, though there they'll often follow the typical patterns of that industry – hence standard industry-models such as eTOM for telecommunications or SCOR for supply-chain operations. Once we get down to tier-3, though, the structure is usually close to unique even within the industry – a complete overview of what the organization does, and how it structures that work.

So if the vision describes what the organization *is*, the function-model describes what the organization *does* – its role within the enterprise-vision. And, like the vision, the role does not change much, if at all, because if it does, it will no longer be the same organization: so *the function-model will stay much the same for as long as the organization does that kind of work*. This means that the function-model is an extremely important document – because when it's placed side-by-side with the vision, we have a "totem-pole to unify the tribes."

Most enterprise-architects would build a function-model via some form of literature-search across the organization, working together with a few key "insider" stakeholders who know the business well. But for this project, we have an almost unique opportunity: the direct engagement of most of the key players in the organization. So here we'll be able to do this as a live workshop, with direct feedback to make sure that we've got it right. We'll only have time to do a two-tier model, but that should be enough for this purpose here; and to make it more engaging, we'll ask each participant to bring a photograph of themselves to place on the model.

That gives us enough to work with for now.

Linking It All Together

This is not an organization that's strong on strategy, and it's still mostly structured into silos and sub-units: that much was clear from the previous workshops. And it's also clear that we need to start from where they are, rather than from where we'd like them to end up. All of which, in turn, suggests an obvious sequence for the workshop, which we duly note in the project-diary:

- start by working with them to develop a two-tier functional business model
- use the "organization and enterprise" diagram to introduce the notion of "enterprise" as an entity to which the organization must relate
- introduce the concept of vision as an active bridge between organization and enterprise, and explain how it relates to respect
- work with them to develop a preliminary vision

We'll also add a strong emphasis on how to identify what a usable vision looks like and feels like, and how to use it in practice, so that they can continue to develop it once the workshop is over.

It'll be a tight squeeze to fit it all into a half-day, but it'll be doable. Ready for tomorrow, then.

Application

- What methodology – or methodologies – do you follow when developing a project-plan for implementation? In what ways does the methodology vary in different domains and for different scales of projects?

- How *do* you decide what you will do in implementing a project-brief? How do you translate down from the abstract brief into concrete detail? How do you select from among all the various options? How do you *find* appropriate options? And how do you decide how to decide?

- How do you know when it's time to stop looking for solutions, and start to implement something? When does the project-plan stop being an abstract "plan" and start to become practical guidance for real work in real-time? And what do you need to do *at the planning-stage* to ensure that the plan can be updated and adapted to changing circumstances during implementation, while still maintaining appropriate governance throughout?

- How would you go about planning a workshop to help an organization find out what it really is and does – the highest level of its enterprise-architecture? What safeguards would you need to build in to ensure that the participants stay on track, and not wander off on well-worn paths such as "not invented here," "not in my job-description," "the way we've always done it," or "the money is all that matters"?

- How would you deliver that workshop? What style would you use: for example, role-play, lecture, games, or other options? Why would you choose those specific options? What outcomes would you expect from using those options?

Summary

In this chapter, we explored how to expand a preliminary solution into a detailed plan for action that can be applied in real-world practice. The solutions discussed are specific to the two projects described in this book; the "Application" section at the end of the chapter provides a broader range of test-questions to use for other types of project in your own context.

The main deliverables here are the detailed plans for action for each project, based on the respective "preliminary solution" approved at the end of the previous day.

In the next chapter, we'll put those plans into action.

CHAPTER 8

Day 8: Putting It into Practice

Here at last we reach the point where things actually *happen* in the real world and – to the delight of business-folk – the real value is delivered. And here, often, one of the main tasks of architecture is to keep out of the way...

In the implementation stage of a conventional large project, the architecture is already supposed to be complete: all that's left is to ensure compliance to the plan. The usual way to do this is via "gateway reviews": at each stage the project-lead presents a formal statement of compliance, the architects review it and make various suggestions, the project-leads change their designs to take note of this masterful advice, and everyone is happy. That's the theory, anyway, even if it doesn't quite work out that way in practice.

One of my first jobs in enterprise-architecture consisted of reviewing project-plans to ensure compliance against "the architecture." To say that we were hated by the developers was perhaps an overstatement, but none of us exactly relished our role as "architecture police"...

We did prove our value, many times over – such as when we found that three projects each wanted to place their own separate and incompatible RFID infrastructures into the same physical space, or when we showed that a tiny "glue-project" would add literally billions of value to the projects that it could link together. But it took us quite a while to realize that we needed to catch these architectural issues *before* they entered the implementation-phase. And for that to work, we needed all the players involved to recognize that architecture is *everyone's* responsibility – not solely that of the architects.

© Tom Graves 2023
T. Graves, *Everyday Enterprise Architecture*, https://doi.org/10.1007/978-1-4842-8904-4_8

We then realized that, to make this happen, we needed to change our role, from that of The Architect (with grandiose capital-letters in the job-title) to proponents and educators of a single *qualitative* idea – the *idea* of architecture.

In essence, all of enterprise-architecture comes down to that one idea:

Things work better when they work together, with clarity, with elegance, on purpose.

There are a fair few frills beyond that bald statement, of course, but that really *is* the point of everything that we do. It's all about *effectiveness*: an overall melding of all of the various factors to arrive at an answer, a solution, a practice, or whatever, that is efficient, reliable, elegant, appropriate, and integrated. That's what we do; that's the "one idea" that we have and can share with everyone else in the enterprise.

Implementation-governance is one of the ways in which we share that "one idea" with others, but it's essential to ensure that it's not the only way that we're seen to do so. Architecture is dynamic, not static; implementation takes *time*, which means that whatever we build our compliance against is going to change over time too. And since many of the best architectural ideas will arise from what happens right down at the point of action, we need to avoid the trap of deluding ourselves into a belief that because we have a better overview than most, we therefore have a better knowledge of everything than most: the plain fact is that we don't. Architecture, and even design, may be a job for generalists, but implementation is a job for specialists – and we forget that fact at our peril.

So while we help other specialists with their implementations, it's useful to ask about *our* specialism, *our* implementation. We may well have specialized in other areas in the past, which means that we should be able to do some of that detail-level design and implementation ourselves. But *as architects*, we would typically describe ourselves as generalists – hence *we specialize in how to be a generalist*. Our specialism is about thinking about how things work together and can work together in better ways, thinking about thinking, thinking about feelings too – anything that will help to make anything in the enterprise more *effective*. That's our practice; that's what *we* implement. And it's useful to keep that in mind during this phase of the architecture cycle, where the focus is on implementation for real results in the real-time world.

Main Project: Implementing Architecture

One of the hardest parts of enterprise-architecture is explaining what we do, and how and why it is of value to the organization. Much of it is as much art or craft as it is science, which often will make it even harder to explain, precisely because it's so personal in nature. And even in those parts of the discipline that look more like science, it's easy to get lost in all the abstractions. Somehow we need to bring it back to that one key point: what do we *do*, and how do we do it?

Hence the project we've been working on for these past few days, which so far has reached the stage of an explicit project-plan:

- Introduce a new conceptual tool for architecture: "Context-space mapping," linking the OODA decision-cycle and SCAN-like sensemaking into the standard architecture-cycle

- Introduce it in the form of text and visuals, using a "soft lines" approach and style for both

- Illustrate systems-principles concepts such as recursion by using the tool itself, and its usage, as its own example

This won't cover all of architecture, of course – only one small part of it, in fact. But it should be enough to help others understand what it is that we do, how we do it, and so on – which is the main point of this exercise.

As we saw earlier, it's really about what building-architects call "meta-thinking," to which we could also add meta-methodology, or even meta-architecture: thinking about thinking, observing the observing, architecting the architecture. Which is abstract. Again. So let's take it out of the abstract and bring it down into the real world of practice.

Pick a context: any context. Something that's of interest to you and your clients. It doesn't even need to be a "problem." Anything will do, though preferably something that you're already working on at present.

If you're like most architects, you'll have started scribbling some ideas on this already, or perhaps roughed out a mind-map, or put up a collection of sticky-notes on a whiteboard. But for now, backtrack for a moment, and go all the way back to the bare canvas. Scribble a shape of some kind. As in Figure 8-1, just call it "the context," as a kind of generic placeholder for whatever kind of context we might be dealing with.

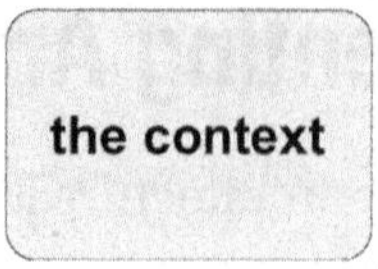

the context

Figure 8-1. *The context*

There's the way we look at that context as a description of a problem that needs to be solved or resolved, which we might describe as "problem-space." And there's the way we look at that context in terms of how we would select a means to resolve that problem, which we might describe as "solution-space." Each of those is actually the flipside of the other, or, more precisely, a *view* into the same context-space. Think of it as two views either side of the same sheet of glass, with the context described in pen-marks on its surface. Or perhaps easier, as two clones of the *same* image that we slide apart on a wall or a whiteboard, as shown in Figure 8-2.

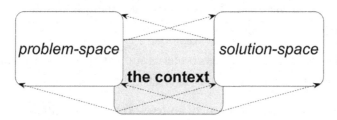

Figure 8-2. *Problem-space and solution-space*

We create an artificial separation between "problem" and "solution" to help us make sense: but it's important to remember that it doesn't actually exist. Neither is there any actual separation between ourselves and the context – that too is something that we invent for our convenience, or sanity, or suchlike. And it's important, too, to remember that we also bring everything of ourselves into that "conversation," including all of our background, our culture, our training, our assumptions, our history: we too are part of that context, *interwoven* with both "problem" and "solution." In effect, we place ourselves as an intermediary between "problem" and "solution," so as to bring them back into convergence again when we've made some kind of sense of what's going on.

"Problem, meet solution; solution, meet problem; let's all go have a chat over a coffee somewhere." May not sound entirely rational, perhaps, but that's actually an important point in itself: this part of the architecture process *isn't* "rational," in fact, by definition *cannot* be "rational," because it *creates* the logic of the space within which the "rationality" of the chosen solution will operate. From chaos we *create* apparent order: it's important to remember that that "order" is merely that which we *choose* to see, often something that we invent, and may not actually exist in the real world at all...

So everything within that context starts off as "the unknown," a near-random collection of facts, figures, and fragments that we acquire by any means available to us. As the sensemaking process begins, it's an unordered, disordered mess: somehow we have to make sense of it, to come to decisions about what to do with it, and then take action. We observe; orient; decide; and act.

One of our options may be to take no action, of course. But ideally that "non-action" needs to be something that we *choose* to not-do, rather than a non-choice made for us by default.

But how does that actually work? We go back to the context again: Observe: what can we see? Orient: what's going on? Decide: what do we do about it? Act: *do* it.

Observe. Orient. Decide. Act. Observe. Orient. Decide. Act. Again. And again. And again. Fast. Faster. And faster. Until we're aware of how it all happens, right here, right now, in real-time.

Enterprise-architecture, in real-time. *Agile* enterprise-architecture.

For architects, the **Observe** part is usually quite easy: we have to be generalists, hence more eclectic than most, and hence more likely to allow more into our awareness. We're also less likely than other disciplines to be rattled by randomness, the apparently "chaotic," with less need for a nominal "reason" before we'll allow something to seem interesting in any given context. In short, we're better than most at dealing with unorder – which definitely helps here.

Given what we've observed, we now have to make sense of what we've observed. We **Orient** our perceptions into some conceptual form, allow meaning to emerge from out of that complexity, as patterns, heuristics, suggestions, implications, guidelines.

As the sensemaking settles down, we need to **Decide** what to do with what we've seen, with what we now understand. No doubt it will seem complicated at first, but with careful thought, careful analysis, we should be able to whittle it all down into some kind of algorithm, a more predictable and certain world.

Which at last brings us something with which we can **Act**. Define the rules for action. Keep it simple. Keep it fast.

Again.

Observe: Watch the "chaos."

Orient: Allow meaning to emerge from the complexity.

Decide: Winnow through all the choices and complications.

Act: bring it down to something simple, right here, right now.

Another iteration; and another: Observe, orient, decide, act. Again. And again. Fast. Faster.

Observe: explore the *Not-known.* Orient: align within the *Ambiguous.* Decide: resolve the *Complicated.* Act: accept the *Simple.* New information arises from the Not-known; Observe it, move to the Ambiguous. New ways of seeing arise in the Ambiguous; Orient to it, move to the Complicated. Complete the sensemaking through analysis in the Complicated, then Decide on Simple rules to Act. Which brings up new information. So there's a double-pattern in there, as that SCAN-style pattern also comes into the picture.

And then another pattern, because there's an oscillation from real-time observation to grabbing a moment or two away from the action to make sense and to decide, then back to real-time again to act and then observe again.

And another oscillation – another loop, as shown in Figure 8-3 – swinging side to side from the uncertain in observation to making sense to bringing some kind of order to take action in terms of that perceived order and back again to the uncertainties that the *real* world shows us.

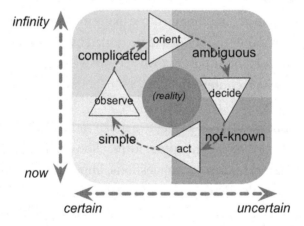

Figure 8-3. *Inner-loop cycle: sensemaking and decision-making*

And another overlay, and another, layers and layers of ways to make sense and take action, all within the same problem-space and solution-space and, at the end, just the context, itself. Being what it *is*, while we interact with it.

Except that decisions made in the moment can have effects that last for decades. Or forever.

Which means that we need to take real care over those decisions, too. In real-time. Yet the closer we get to real-time, the fewer options we have to reflect, to analyze, and to experiment – hence we may seem all but forced to choose between Not-known and Simple, because, as shown in Figure 8-4, that's all that's left when the timescale becomes that compressed. And if we're not able to accept "chaos" of the Not-known for what it is, we may end up trying to "take control" of something that, by definition, cannot be controlled. Which is not a good idea...

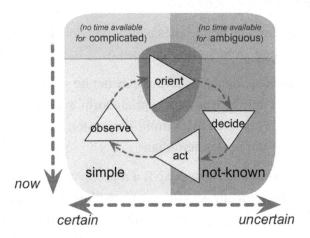

Figure 8-4. *Time-compression in the OODA real-time cycle*

So we need to find some way to create "time to think," even when there's almost no time available to think – certainly none for the usual "analysis paralysis" of conventional enterprise-architecture.

Which is where and why these *context-space maps* come into the story, because they provide a way to skim through many different views onto a context fast enough to help make sense in architectural terms in near-real-time.

Base-Maps and Cross-Maps

Context-space maps have two distinct components: a *base-map*, which provides a common frame of reference for a set of context-space maps; and any number of *cross-maps* that provide alternate views and categories for sensemaking in the same context. The typical characteristics for a good base-map would include:

- *Universality*: It covers the entire scope of a given context – in principle, anyway

- *Sensemaking*: Its purpose is to guide sensemaking and decision-support, rather than design and implementation of a specific "solution"

- *Simple partitioning*: It divides the context into a small number of regions or "domains" (typically four or five), and often including a "none-of-the-above" region (such as the central region of "Reality" in the framework we've used here)

- *Fluid boundaries*: The boundaries between regions may be allowed to move, blur, and/or be somewhat porous

- *Usage-independent layout*: Its layout may not be semantically significant, and may take any appropriate form, such as a horizontal or vertical single-dimension, or multi-dimensional form such as the four-axis/three-dimension tetradian

In systems-theory terms, each base-map is a *rotation* that provides multiple views into the same overall space. Ideally we also want it to illustrate the balance in the context (*reciprocation* and *resonance*), and preferably the layering (*recursion* and *reflexion*) in that context too.

As we've seen previously, perhaps the most useful base-map for sensemaking is one that categorizes the context in terms of cause-effect relationships and repeatability:

- *Simple*: Presumed absolute repeatability – perceived cause-effect linkage is linear and direct

- *Complicated*: Presumed repeatable – perceived relationship between cause and effect is linear but "complicated," often with delays and feedback-loops

- *Ambiguous*: Repeatability is uncertain – "cause" and "effect" are intertwined and interdependent (an "effect" becomes part of input to its own "cause" in the next iteration)

- *Not-known*: Not repeatable – no discernible cause-effect relationships

- *"Reality"*: "None-of-the-above" region, before cause-effect categorization has taken place

Which leads us to the base-frame shown in Figure 8-5, as a means to describe an overall context – whether as "problem" or as "solution."

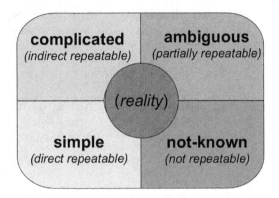

Figure 8-5. *Suggested base-frame for context-space maps*

Another enterprise-architecture colleague also pointed out that much the same could be said about the fluidity of the boundaries between the domains themselves, leading to another recursion:

- *Simple boundaries*: The boundaries between the domains are fixed, explicit, and absolute ("either/or")

- *Complicated boundaries*: The boundaries between the domains are explicit and absolute, but can move somewhat along each axis (as in a finite and discrete spectrum, or in the way that IT can make analytic decision-making faster, and hence "closer" to real-time)

- *Ambiguous boundaries*: The boundaries between the domains may blur (such as where one or both of the axes are a "both/and" spectrum rather than a strict "either/or" distinction)

- *Not-known boundaries*: The boundaries are quantum-like – they both exist *and* do not exist, all in the same moment

One of the problems is that all the arbitrary layerings of cross-maps can provide multiple meanings for the same base-map – sometimes even within the same diagram – which, if we're not careful, can create plenty of opportunity for confusion. A context-map is not "true" as such: it's simply a way to look at a context, a *tool* to help us make sense fast. For example, if we use that preceding base-map, we might decide to add overlays for layers of abstraction, for timescale, and for a spectrum of interpretation-types – which would give us a context-map like that shown in Figure 8-6.

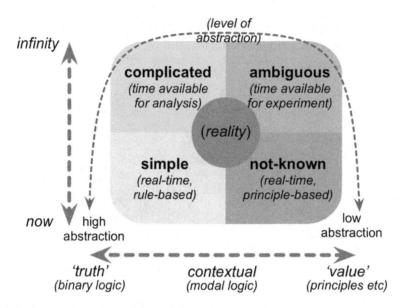

Figure 8-6. *Timescales versus interpretations*

To expand a bit on the dimensions of that map:

- The base-map tells us our range of views when dealing with the real world (Simple, Complicated, Ambiguous, and Not-known).

- The "layers of abstraction" scale is actually an analogue of perceived repeatability, but it also warns us how much we may risk over-simplifying our view of the context.

- The "horizontal" axis ("value" versus "truth") is a spectrum of interpretation, ranging from a binary true/false in terms of predefined "objective truth" at one end (extreme of Complicated/Simple) to almost completely subjective and therefore necessarily principle-based at the other end (extreme of Ambiguous/Not-known).

- The "vertical" axis ("infinity" versus "now") is a spectrum of time available for decision-making, ranging from apparently infinite (such as we see in the Complicated-domain "analysis-paralysis" and its Ambiguous-domain equivalents) to a real-time "Now!" (where there may literally only be split-seconds in which to make an appropriate decision).

What this really tells us is that Ambiguous-domain experiments and Complicated-domain analysis are a kind of luxury that depend on having time available for prolonged decision-making. The closer we get to real-time action, the more we're forced into a narrow band where we have to keep things very simple: either follow the rules, or follow the principles, with no time for anything elaborate.

In that sense, the Simple and Not-known domains have some strong similarities. In decision-making terms, the only real choice along that line is in the extent to which a decision is objective ("truth"-based) or subjective ("value"-based). In the Simple case, we assume that context and actions alike are predictable, controllable; in the Not-known case, neither context nor actions can be predicted, while "control" exists only as a myth, a distant delusion. And somewhere in the middle, between these two extremes, is *this* context, right here, right now.

Given this, we then need to work out which of those approaches is most appropriate for the context. To do this, we again use the base-frame, but this time in its consistent usage to map degrees of repeatability in the underlying "problem-space." Which tells us, for example:

- Lower apparent repeatability places us in the Ambiguous or Not-known domain for decision-making (via "value"-based decisions)

- High apparent repeatability places us in the Complicated/Simple pairing (via "truth"-based decisions)

- Low repeatability and limited time (the Not-known domain) means that we must have appropriate principles in place to guide real-time decision-making – which we would typically derive from experiments in the Ambiguous-domain

- Limited time but high-repeatability (the Simple domain) depends on the availability of appropriate rules – as in ISO9000-style "work-instructions" – that would typically be derived from Complicated-domain analysis

The context-map shows us that the combination of repeatability (in the problem-space) and the compression of time available for decision-making (in "solution-space") will force us into this fairly straightforward split in decision-making choices.

The base-diagram in Figure 8-5 is one of the most versatile base-maps for enterprise-architecture, but there are many others we might use. For example, there's the five-element lifecycle map shown in Figure 8-7, which we can link to specific time-perspectives, and also cross-link recursively to the five themes of effectiveness.

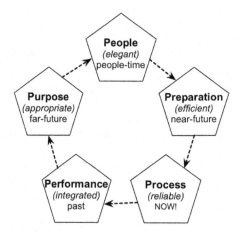

Figure 8-7. *Five-elements, effectiveness and time*

We can use this to give us many different intersecting views on a context, such as:

- What parts of this context deal with Purpose, or Process, or Performance?

- Where does this context focus on the far-future, near-future, immediate-present, or past?

- Where does this context deal with the fluidity of "people-time," swinging almost at random along a spectrum from far-past to far-future?

- What aspects of the context emphasize efficiency, or human-factors, or overall integration?

- How would we make our strategy (Purpose) in this context more "green" (efficient – "optimizes overall use of resources")?

- How should human-factors ("elegance") support our operational (Process) tactics (Preparation, recursively)?

Metaphorically speaking, we "walk around" within the base-map, pulling in various cross-maps as overlays in whatever way seems to make sense, to build up a conceptual picture of what's going in the context. Recursion occurs when we use the base-map as a cross-map on itself – such as when looking at Preparation *within* a Process, in that preceding example.

Another example of that kind of recursion occurs when we look at relationships between data, information, knowledge, and wisdom. These are usually shown as a vertical "stack," with lowly data at the base and wisdom as perfection at the top. But if we explore that "stack" using the base-frame, some interesting cross-comparisons appear, as we can see in Figure 8-8.

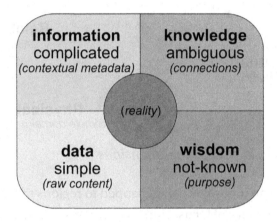

Figure 8-8. *Data, information, knowledge, wisdom*

From this, we can see that the vertical-stack notion is misleading: it's more accurate to say that they each represent distinct *regions* or *dimensions* of the conceptual space. So, for example, it's entirely correct that we have discrete data-management, knowledge-management, and information-management; and it's no joke to say that we'll also need something resembling wisdom-management, because we may well have "wisdom-like" items, such as purported "best practices." These need to be managed in their own right, yet actually make no practical sense until anchored into the real world via concrete data and contextual metadata, and then connected into the *personalized* knowledge that can be gained only through personal experience.

A recursion here is that data, information, and the like are only one dimension – the "conceptual dimension" – in the set of asset-types we explored earlier with the segment-model framework: physical, such as "things"; conceptual, such as information;

relational, such as links between people; and aspirational, such as purpose, or morale, or the somewhat abstract link that's represented by a brand. These are *dimensions*, rather than regions that can be mapped directly onto a two-dimensional surface, so it's often best to show them in a *tetradian* format, as the four internal axes of a tetrahedron shown in Figure 8-9.

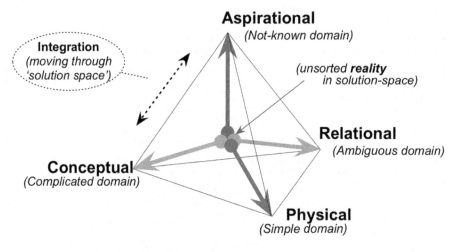

Figure 8-9. Asset-types as tetradian dimensions

Those dimensions can in turn be cross-mapped to regions of repeatability, or, for example, to the different types of focus within a business context, as shown in Figure 8–10 on a simple cardboard tetrahedral version of the same model.

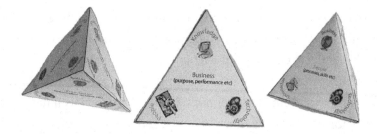

Figure 8-10. Cardboard-model tetradian, rotated

As we saw earlier, most actual business-assets are combinations of these dimensions: a paper form is both a physical "thing" and an information-object, which in turn may represent a relational-asset such as via a signature. Hence it's useful to think of assets – and also functions, locations, capabilities, even events – as occupying a *region* within that tetradian space. Decision-types, and skill-types in capabilities, will often need to use a different set of dimensions: the underlying concept is essentially the same as for assets, but it's probably easiest to describe in a base-diagram layout, as shown in Figure 8-11.

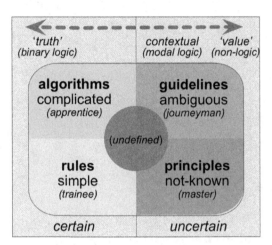

Figure 8-11. *Decision-types and base-diagram domains*

Much the same would apply if we use the segment-model framework as a context-space map: the cells within the framework represent dimensional "primitives," but most real-world entities are "composites" that straddle across rows, columns, or segments, or any combination of those. Yet once we understand that they *are* composites, we can then drill-down as appropriate, back to the respective base-primitives of the segment-model, as shown in Figure 8-12 – which is one of the key themes that enables architectural redesign.

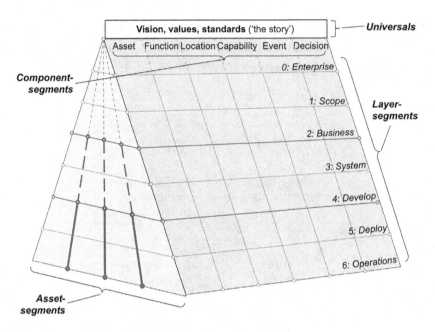

Figure 8-12. *Segment-model framework as base-map*

Another valuable base-map is the "business-model canvas," shown in Figure 8-13, and first presented by Alex Osterwalder, Yves Pigneur, and others in the book *Business Model Generation*. If used solely at the business-architecture level, it provides us with a bit more detail to extend the basic tier-1 functional business-model, by summarizing who does what and why in the organization's internal and external relationships.

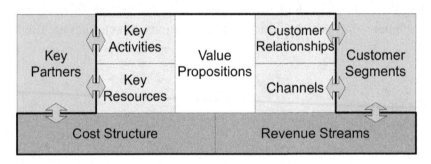

Figure 8-13. *Business Model Canvas*

That's at a whole-organization level, assuming explicit boundaries between the organization and its partners on one side, and its customers on the other. But if we think of it as an *enterprise* model rather than a whole-organization one, we can apply the same recursion as for the enterprise-scope model, because *every* part of the organization

- Has customers for whom it needs to present value-propositions, with whom it needs to maintain relationships and communicate through channels, and who contribute either directly or indirectly to its revenue-streams.

- Has suppliers, service-providers, and other partners who share in its key activities and provide or interact with its key resources, and who interact with its cost-structures.

The meanings of "customer," "partner," "value," "revenue," and "cost" will all vary with the context, but the principle remains the same in every part of the enterprise – hence a very useful set of tests to assess the context.

Given a set of base-maps such as these, we then need to collect a stack of cross-maps in our conceptual toolkit, to act as "flip-cards" to scan through many different views onto a context. We've seen quite a few so far, and you'll also find some others – most of them overlaid on the main base-map – in Appendix B, later in the book.

I guess we might be in some danger of getting lost in theory at this point, so it'd be wise to throw in a reminder that the key driver here, *always*, is about finding ways to make sense of the context, and apply it in practice, *fast*. The theory may be fascinating, but sometimes so in an all-too-literal sense: we need to remember that our clients in the business and elsewhere are no doubt waiting impatiently for real results – and we'd better deliver.

Yet engaging others in this type of exploration *is* a key part of our work as architects, promoting, expressing and enacting that "one idea": "things work better when they work together, with clarity, with elegance, on purpose." We do *need* the right level of theory in order to provide the proper foundations to explain those ideas in practice: the trick here is in finding the right balance.

Problem-Space and Solution-Space

To make it practical, we need to *link* theory to practice in a way that also links "problem" to "solution." One way to do this is to create maps of "solution-space" that position various pre-packaged options for action – "solutions" – onto the *same* base-maps and cross-maps that we've used to assess the "problem-space." When the two types of maps align, the process of scanning through problem-space will automatically indicate options for action – and usually with the same characteristics of recursion and the like, such that the same "solution" can be used in many different ways and in many different layers and aspects of the organization.

For example, as shown in Figure 8-14, we could start with the five-element lifecycle-model with the overlay of the five dimensions of effectiveness applied recursively onto that, as described earlier, to give us a context-space map with which to assess the respective problem-space.

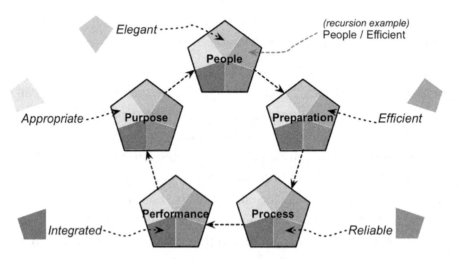

Figure 8-14. *Effectiveness and the five-element lifecycle*

With this map, we would typically aim to identify where problem-areas might be: such as the people-side of planning, perhaps, and a general lack of awareness of direction of the organization, which we might describe in those terms as Purpose/ Elegant. A matching solution-map will list various options for action against the *same* categories, such that the process of "walking around" in problem-space also automatically becomes a means to identify appropriate options to address the respective issues. For example, we could take that preceding cross-map of the effectiveness-dimensions and five-element lifecycle, and then cross-map again to a set of example "solutions" for each region within the context-space map:

Purpose *themes*: identity, morale, brand awareness

- *Purpose/Efficient*: Vision/values as "credo" for decision-making

- *Purpose/Reliable*: Emphasis on principles with rules as default

- *Purpose/Elegant*: Use of emotive language to enhance engagement

- *Purpose/Appropriate*: Explicit reference to "outside" contexts (vision/role/mission/goals layering); whole-of-context standards – ISO-14000, ISO-17000, etc.

- *Purpose/Integrated*: Whole-of-organization strategy development

People *themes*: satisfaction, conflict resolution

- *People/Efficient*: Privacy; reputation-management; "Cluetrain" tactics; leadership development

- *People/Reliable*: Integrity/ethics training; shift to win/win perspective

- *People/Elegant*: CRM and social-CRM systems; customer-relationship training; work/life balance; accessibility, ergonomics, and personalization

- *People/Appropriate*: Customer-value analysis; principle-based employment/stakeholder-relationships

- *People/Integrated*: Customer-centric operating-models; "wholeness responsibility"

Preparation *themes*: knowledge audit, capability assessment, gap analysis

- *Preparation/Efficient*: Capability development, innovation training, systems thinking; explicit "development time"

- *Preparation/Reliable*: Knowledge-management (KM); knowledge audit/review; integrated performance-support systems (IPSS)

- *Preparation/Elegant*: Tacit KM – communities of practice, "Yellow Pages" skills/expertise directories, weblogs

- *Preparation/Appropriate*: Knowledge audit; gap-analysis

- *Preparation/Integrated*: Intranet/extranet, social-media, and other shared KM; security policy/review

Process *themes*: resources, skills-base, operating environment

- *Process/Efficient*: Active learning (e.g., After Action Review); kaizen continuous improvement; supply-chain analysis

- *Process/Reliable*: Workflow analysis; capability analysis; scenario development; risk/opportunity analysis

- *Process/Elegant*: Post-compliance TQM (e.g., quality circles); occupational health and safety (OH&S); ergonomics, personalization, IPSS

- *Process/Appropriate*: Strategic review – SWOT, SCORE, etc.; large-group interventions (e.g., Open Space, Future Search)

- *Process/Integrated*: ISO-9000:2000; post-compliance TQM

Performance *themes*: benchmarks, scorecards, dashboards

- *Performance/Efficient*: Benchmarking; real-time dashboards; integration frameworks

- *Performance/Reliable*: Enterprise-wide dashboards; interactive intranet/extranet (e.g., wiki, chat, conferencing, social-media); narrative and dialogue; large-group interventions (e.g., Open Space)

- *Performance/Elegant*: Equity/diversity policy and practice; complexity-system techniques

- *Performance/Appropriate*: Real-time dashboards; performance in relation to maturity-models; values/performance review

- *Performance/Integrated*: SEMPER; Extended Balanced Scorecard; Triple Bottom Line; GRI; AA1000

These aren't "solutions" as such, but they do represent approaches that line up conceptually with the respective issues and have been proven to work in real-life usage. As with all architecture, though, it will usually need some interpretation, for which we could again apply the usual context-space mapping:

- *Simple*: The "solution" is proven best-practice and should work well in this context without any change – for example, a work-instruction for cleaning kitchen floors in a fast-food franchise.

- *Complicated*: The "solution" is proven good-practice and should work well when certain known factors are calibrated to the context – for example, setup configurations to install a server on a wide variety of system-types and operating-systems.

- *Ambiguous*: The "solution" is a pattern that has been observed to appear to work in contexts of this type, and could be a good starting-point for experimentation – for example, creating a community-of-practice to enhance skills-sharing.

- *Not-known*: The "solution" probably makes sense in this context as a trigger for appropriate action, if used as a means to focus on overall guiding principles – for example, creating ideas for business-innovation.

There are always variations: for example, in the Chaotic case, we might deliberately choose the exact inverse of the options that are suggested in the solution-map, to see if we could trigger off an "immune-system" type of response. That's where the skill of the architect really comes into play – and also why it takes a lot of careful practice over a *long* time to develop those skills without causing a lot of damage along the way...

So, in a sense, it's good that most enterprise-architects start out in IT-architecture, because most of what happens there is in "ordered" contexts – from very-Simple to very-Complicated – that provide a good base for skills-development before tackling any of the genuinely Ambiguous or Not-known "uncertainty" contexts.

The true complexities of business-politics and the like can cause real difficulties for many of the would-be architects coming up from IT, but in practice it can actually be much harder to come the other way, from business to IT. Simple-domain contexts follow strict invariant rules, often with no room for negotiation – a fact that many business-folk will find immensely frustrating – and the sheer volume of simple detail needed to make something work well can be utterly overwhelming if we're not used to it.

In short, there are very good reasons why successful enterprise-architects tend to be going somewhat grey in places by the time they really hit their stride!

Both "problem" and "solution" are ways of looking at the context: they aren't separate from the context, nor are they really separate from each other. In a very real sense, as architects, we *are* "the problem," just as much as we are "the solution," the initial means by which the desired change will come about. But how do we describe that, in a way that makes sense to anyone else? We're going to need a good metaphor.

One metaphor we might use is the answer to the old physics question of "is light waves or particles?" It turns out that the closest to a correct answer to that question is "yes, therefore no": "wave" and "particle" represent different ways to *interpret* the phenomena of light, but ultimately neither can describe what light really *is*. If we describe light in terms of particles, we can understand certain ways that light behaves, such as photoelectric effects and so on. If we describe light as waves, we can explain *other* ways that light behaves, but which particles can't do – such as light's ability to move through solid glass. Both views are "true" in their own way, but each of them contradicts the other, so we can only make sense of what's going on by using only *one* of those views at a time.

The important point, though, is that we can *do* different things with each view that the other view won't let us do. If we choose a useful set of views, *and then switch between them as we need,* we can cover a much broader *overall* scope, and still make sense of what's going on. Consider a light-bulb, for example. We'd typically say that the light comes out of the light-source as photons, or particles of light. But particles can't get through the glass, so we'd switch to saying that light is made up of waves. Switching metaphors like this is a bit of a crazy trick, but it *works*.

Switching between metaphors is also the core to how we use context-space mapping: it's not that there is a single view that is "the truth," but that we switch between metaphors to give us different view on that context, and to allow us to make sense of what we see. We then use that sensemaking to guide subsequent decision-making, about what we should do within that context to achieve the results we want. And in the same way, we collapse the supposed separation between "problem" and "solution" to arrive at our choice of action. Making sense, making decisions; observe, orient, decide, act.

So how does this work in practice? At its simplest, as shown in Figure 8-15, we go for a walk – metaphorically speaking – around the "world" described by the context-space map and by what we ourselves observe in the context itself. We begin with any appropriate base-map that seems to fit, or that gives us a useful-seeming place to start, and then add or remove cross-map overlays to give us new questions with which to orient ourselves to what's going on. Perhaps we might switch over to another base-map, start again from there – all in a matter of minutes. But in essence, that's it: we go for a walk – all over the map, in whatever way makes sense.

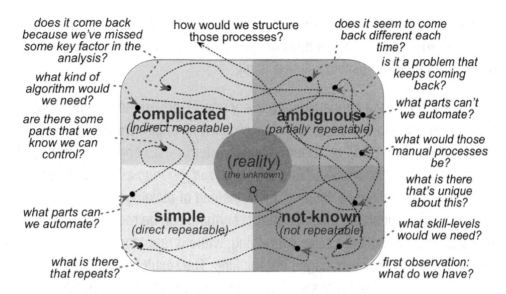

Figure 8-15. *Walk through the context*

Relevant aspects may be scattered all over the map, or occupy multiple regions within the map – there's no set rule that says that there will only be one region of interest or concern within the context. And in the same way, different segments of a problem may need different matching solutions: some parts may be Simple, if we're lucky, but others may well be Ambiguous in the extreme, and we'll need to address *all* of those aspects in some way or other in order to achieve real lasting success.

This, incidentally, is one more reason why describing IT-architecture as "enterprise-architecture" is so dangerous: it views the entire context from an IT-specific viewpoint, and hence ignores anything that cannot be made to fit an IT-centric "solution." Which, yes, can work quite well – sometimes – when the scope is restricted solely to the "worlds" inside of IT-boxes; *but it does not and cannot work with any true real-world context* that reaches beyond those artificially Simple constraints.

The blunt reality is that IT systems in general can only handle Simple problems well, and Complicated problems only at ever-increasing expense and fragility, but are often worse than useless in the inherently uncertain domains of deep-Ambiguous and Not-known. Yet most real-world contexts will include aspects in *all* domains: for example, every real business-system will include Ambiguous human processes alongside any automated Simple or Complicated ones. A "solution" that only handles the Simple parts of any context and dumps everything else into the "too-hard basket" is no usable solution at all.

But that's exactly what's happened with every new IT-driven fad. Whenever a new idea comes along – such as business process re-engineering (BPR), service-oriented architecture (SOA), or "cloud"-based systems – IT vendors rush to build some pre-packaged "solution" around that idea, *but ignoring all those aspects of the context that cannot be "solved" by IT.* Instead of tackling the context as a whole, the vendors push the delusion that everything can be reduced to Simple rules, enabling automation to solve everything, without requiring any change to management models or management thinking. The result has usually been an expensive failure: *very* expensive. As one of the originators of BPR, Michael Hammer, put it, "I was reflecting my engineering background and was insufficiently appreciative of the human dimension. I've learned that that's critical."

Ignoring the human dimensions of a context *does not work*. Most of "the human dimension" sits firmly within the Ambiguous domain – and we *cannot* "solve" that with a Simple IT-system. Which is why our enterprise-architecture *must* be a true "architecture of the enterprise" – and not solely "the architecture of the enterprise-IT."

We keep walking, keep walking, round and round within the context-space map, building up a kind of holographic impression of the overall context, exploring some parts in fine detail, others only skimmed-over, and using recursion and reflexion to fill in the conceptual gaps, switching back and forth between "observe" and "orient," between "problem" and "solution." Then at some point - often without apparent warning, though sometimes because we simply run out of time to do any more exploring - we know it's time to stop exploring, and *decide*.

That moment of decision is what triggers and enables *action*.

And that's the point our clients have been waiting for all along: that's where *they* gain concrete value from our work. That's often also the point where the responsibility passes out of our hands, and into the hands of others - the designers, the engineers, the specialist solution-architects, and others, who will put those understandings that we've gained about the context to practical *use*. Yet for us, as *enterprise*-architects, the story continues on: every new piece of architecture-work will add another layer, another view, into our "holograph" of the enterprise as a whole. Observe, orient, decide, act, is a continuous cycle: *act* must always lead to *observe* once more.

So while others may be more interested at first in the outward results of our work, to us, it's always that continuing *journey* of architectural discovery that matters most. Over time, "problem" and "solution" slowly cease to be separate; it may be true that "the map is not the territory," yet more and more we reach toward a sense in which the context-space map *is* the territory, the means through which we interact with the context of the enterprise itself.

And as Matthew Frederick put it in *101 Things*, "our experience of architectural space is influenced by how we arrive": the journey *is* the architecture, the experience *is* the process. We set out on that journey each time we "take a walk" through context-space; the act of "taking a walk" with others, in an Agile-style architecture, may often be the only intervention that's actually needed. And it's a journey that we aim to share with others, each time we uphold that notion that "things work better when they work together, with clarity, with elegance, on purpose."

So that's context-space mapping: an architectural version of the OODA cycle, where "problem" and "solution" are both embedded within an architectural context. Try it: see what happens. Observe; orient; decide; and act.

In the meantime, though, we still need to see how some of this works in real-world practice, out there with the bank, and what to do about their lost respect.

Example Project: Vision and Function for the Bank

Straight in to the bank's offsite, early in the morning. It's at a large country-club, open, airy, spacy and, of course, expensive: money may be tight these days, but still plenty to be found for the usual executive perks. The room we've been assigned is part of a large banqueting-suite, and the facilities-staff are still tidying up from last night's wedding when we get there. All's fine, though; plenty enough space. Several whiteboards, chairs arranged in clusters around circular tables. A quick refresh on our project-plan:

- Start by working with them to develop a two-tier functional business model.

- Use the "organization and enterprise" diagram to introduce the notion of "enterprise" as an entity to which the organization must relate.

- Introduce the concept of vision as an active bridge between organization and enterprise, and explain how it relates to respect.

- Work with them to develop a preliminary vision.

We drag the tables off to the side, rearranging the chairs into one big circle, with all the whiteboards round the outside. The CEO may not like this layout – he likes to be certain of his position as head of a hierarchy – but we will *need* everyone to be viewed as equals here if this kind of process is going to work. While the facilities staff are out of the room, we quickly transfer all the tea-things onto the circular tables, and pull the big rectangular tables as a block into an open space at one end of the room, two tables wide, three long. It's big enough for everyone to get round, yet still small enough for anyone to reach across to the middle. We cover it with flipchart paper, taped together as a single sheet, and finish the setup just as the first participants start to wander in through the door.

Functional Business Model

This time, for once, they do all seem to arrive reasonably close to time, and have actually taken the no-phones critique to heart – even the CEO is more willing to play by that rule. Some of that previous message about the nature of respect seems to be sinking in: a very good sign, if so.

We start by explaining the role and value of a function-model, as an overview that will get everyone literally "on the same page." So what *does* each person do? What function does their team serve within the organization? And how does that function relate with all the other functions in the organization?

We use the "generic tier-1 function model" in Figure 8-16 to illustrate the basic idea of how the model fits together.

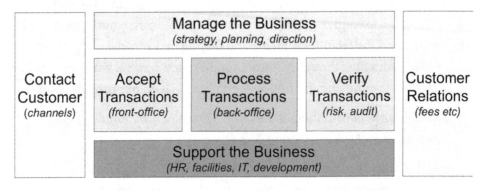

Figure 8-16. *Generic tier-1 functional business model for banking*

And we explain that what we're after here is just the tier-2 model – the basic sub-categories in each of the tier-1 regions, for the bank. We'll do this at first with sticky-notes, placed on the large sheet on that big table off to one side.

We've already provided a base-layout for them, derived in part from the eTOM telecoms-industry standard – deliberately "wrong" for banking, so as to encourage the participants to think more carefully about what they do. As we'd hoped, the model comes together very quickly, almost without argument, showing distinct regions such as strategy, call-centers, risk-management, compliance, trading, back-office, clearing, branch-operations, and IT.

To make it more personal, we say, we'll ask each person to place their own photograph in the respective place on the model. This creates much laughter, as there'd been some confusion about the instructions, hence some people have brought photographs of themselves as children. Others, of course, have forgotten to bring any photograph at all: one woman sketches out a surprisingly good cartoon of herself and uses that instead. We also come across a more interesting problem, because many of the participants have roles that are scattered across many functions in the organization, we have to find a photocopier to churn out various duplicates as required.

After about an hour, the model looks remarkably complete: a very clear picture of what actually happens in the organization, and who is responsible for what. We all lift it carefully up off the table, hang it from the high cross-beam rafters of the room, and stand back to see what else it can show us.

Two points come instantly to mind. One is that people's roles are structured according to their geographic location, their position in the hierarchy, or which of the two banks they used to belong to, or almost anything, it seems, than their actual responsibilities in terms of business function. Which may be why there's so much miscommunication and so many clashes of authority, because almost every function has three or four or even five people with "exclusive" responsibility. Except for one crucial business-function: information-technology.

That's the other key point: the CIO is conspicuously alone, the sole photograph in a large blank area of the canvas, with no-one else to share any of those responsibilities. So even the function-model shows that she has no real support at all: no wonder that she seems so overloaded... The laughter quietly fades all round: there are some thoughtful faces, even shocked faces, standing in front of that model as we move into the morning break. But there are also conversations starting to happen that have never happened before – creating new links across the whole organization, and creating new respect for each other too.

Enterprise-architecture, in action, in real-time, delivering real business-value, right here, right now.

Once the Functional Business Model is in place – and preferably developed to a more-detailed tier-3 level – there's a whole lot more you can do with it. At Australia Post, we used it for mapping projects, to identify gaps and overlaps; the financial team used it for Activity Based Costing; and just about every manager had printed out their own copy and used it for onboarding of new staff and all manner of other things, including as a visual telephone-directory. Others have used it for mapping pain-points and compliance responsibilities. It's one of the most useful architectural models there is, and every new architecture-team should develop their own as one of their very first tasks.

Visioning

We start the second session by drawing a much smaller version of that function-model in the center of a large whiteboard, and then expand it out to show all the key layers of the extended-enterprise: partners and suppliers, clients, prospects and competitors, and government and the broader community, as shown on Figure 8-17.

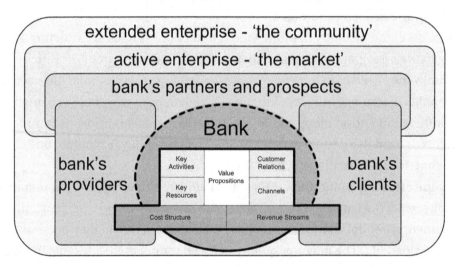

Figure 8-17. *Bank in context of the enterprise*

That, we explain, is the enterprise that they're *actually* working with – *not* solely the "enterprise" of the bank itself. Which leads to the notion of a "vision" that bridges right across the whole of that context, linking the bank with every aspect of its enclosing enterprise. A ***Vision*** is a single, simple phrase that provides the people who comprise "the bank" with a reason to get up in the morning, and that also gives others a clear reason as to why they should relate with the bank. It's about the whole enterprise – not just the bank itself.

Respect is about being "on purpose" for *everyone* involved in the enterprise. And that vision of purpose is also where respect comes from. A full audit-trail where every activity at any time anywhere in the bank links to a goal, to a mission or capability, to the role of the bank within that shared enterprise, to the vision that defines *why* that enterprise exists. And all the way back down again: vision, role, mission, goal, and thence to each and every activity. And, as also shown in Figure 8-18, the vision provides the ultimate anchor for everything that the organization is and does.

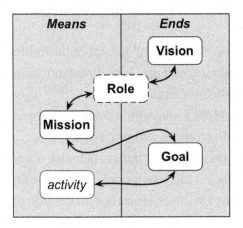

Figure 8-18. *Vision, role, mission, goal*

The vision itself is a short, simple statement describing a "world" desired by all participants in the enterprise. The statement is chosen by the organization itself, but as a means to describe the ecosystem in which it operates, and the *reason* why the various business-relationships and other relationships would exist within that enterprise. For example, Australian brewers Lion Nathan hold to a vision of "a more sociable world," while the IT-industry standards-body Open Group maintain the vision of "boundaryless information-sharing," linked to their tag-line of "making standards work."

Where most attempts at defining a vision go wrong is that they're literally self-centered, describing the enterprise only from the perspective of the organization itself: the classic marketing-style "vision" of "to be the best this-that-or-the-other." To work properly as an anchor for everything the organization is and does, the vision needs to be *much* broader, describing a "world" with space enough for all the other players too. The organization then chooses one or more roles within that "world," as providers of some of the services of that "world," and consumers of others; and the other participants choose their own differing roles, perhaps as "clients" or other service-consumers, perhaps as competitors delivering the same kinds of services, perhaps as regulators, and so on. Yet, in effect, *all* of the active participants and other stakeholders will share at least some aspect of the vision – which is *why* they are stakeholders in that vision. The vision provides the common reference-point that links all those services together.

And a vision itself is not something that can be measured, or "achieved": it just *is*.

It's *stable* – it never changes.

It's *singular* and *universal* – there is only one vision, applying to everything the enterprise is and does.

It's *emotive* – it describes "the passion," it implies desirable or undesirable characteristics for hiring policies, and provides direct motivation, in the sense of "it's what gets me out of bed in the morning."

And it's *strategic* – it provides a focus-point to identify "weak signals" that forewarn of strategic changes in technology, society, and the like.

The vision for the enterprise cannot change, because doing so would fundamentally change the enterprise. (In fact, if the vision *does* change, the enterprise could literally cease to exist – and may take out the organization in the process.) And the vision is not abstract: it needs to appeal in a very *personal* way – and if we can't connect with it in that literally emotive sense of "getting us out of bed in the morning," we're possibly in the wrong enterprise.

For the other nodes in that "audit-trail," the **Role** describes what the organization aims to do *and not do* within the vision's "world," as the ways in which it contributes toward the vision. Although a role-statement may often include some kind of boundary, such as processes, overall activities, or geographical constraints, there's no explicit qualifier, no "best of," "premier provider of," or suchlike – it's just a simple statement about what the organization *does* in this role. And by placing this boundary around what the organization does, this automatically implies other roles that would be needed to realize the vision: for example, if Lion Nathan sees itself in the role of "brewer and distributor" for "a more sociable world," the *other* roles it might need to connect with would include not just the obvious ones such as "customer," "supplier," and "competitor," but others such as "educator in safe and healthy sociability" and even "provider of police services." Taking a whole-of-enterprise view makes it clear that these odder intersections with other roles would be an *expected* part of business – which can "surface" hidden opportunities, and reduce the potential for unpleasant surprises from unexpected stakeholders.

A *Mission* is a description of a capability or service that we will create and then maintain indefinitely thereafter. (Think "trade-mission," rather than one-off military-style mission – in fact the latter is really a type of goal.) So a "mission-statement" should be a straightforward description of the overall means – the *how* – by which a role will be delivered, and of what determines "success" in that role. Each mission must identifiably support a role and vision, and *must* be measurable in some way, because while the mission is never actually "achieved," we need some means to identify the extent of its success. And in many cases, missions are as much about partners, other roles in the Vision-world, because these are the points of contact with these "outside" roles: the metrics for the mission must also monitor and manage that association. Each mission is also a locus for continuous-improvement processes, its metrics that are key inputs for quality-management; and missions also need regular review, not only in relation to their own metrics, but also to the respective role, because each may change the other.

Finally, a *Goal* describes a "project" with a specific set of activities, deliverables, and target date for completion. (Every transit through a value-chain is a kind of "project" with a finite goal.) Each goal contributes toward a mission – it never exists in isolation – and each will be immediate, explicit, concrete, and practical, providing clear boundaries of time, space, and context to make it easier to concentrate on the task to hand. Goals also differ from missions in that, at the end of the project-lifecycle, a goal *completes*, but a mission *continues*; and we measure or review *after* a goal, but *during* a mission. Well-constructed goals can also provide a useful sense of urgency, of *need* to complete.

That brief wander through theory brings us back to the urgent goal here, which is to find some kind of anchor that will re-link the bank with its market, and start to reclaim the lost respect.

We remind the participants here of the role and aims of a vision, in terms of relationships between the organization and enterprise, and emphasize some key themes, of which the most important is Visioning Rule #1: *this is not a marketing exercise!* A pitch is a short-term appeal to the market, while the Vision is the unchanging anchor for the organization itself: it's essential *never* to confuse these two functions, because mistaking a market-pitch for a vision can kill a company – and often has.

The key point is that *the vision never changes*. Strategies and tactics implement the paths toward the vision, and positioning relative to others who connect to the same vision: we use strategy to review the continuous subtle changes needed in the role, and create and maintain missions to match; and we use tactics to define the goals and activities that are needed to support each mission. Successful strategies depend on clear goals and the like; and goals in turn depend on clear missions, roles, and vision. But *a misframed vision will render strategy unreliable, unstable, and error-prone*. Hence getting the vision right is important in the extreme.

Because it's not so much a choice as a *feeling*, identifying a valid vision does take time. Unfortunately we don't have much time here in this workshop, but we should have enough to get a sense of what a workable vision would feel like.

None of this is complicated, though we need to be aware that what we're searching for is not an "idea," but needs to be emotive in some sense: for example, when we've found something that works, it should bring out an almost indignant response of "we do that because *that's who we are!*" And we can make a solid start here, looking for hints of it in the organization's history, in the anecdotes and stories people tell each other, and in the real values that people express in their work. But in the process, we need to be wary of the pitfalls created by some common visioning mistakes:

- *Role as "vision"*: "providers of financial services" – This confuses ends and means, and invites a "so what?" response

- *Mission as "vision"*: "achieve and maintain 30% market share" – This leaves no room for connection with customers, partners, or other stakeholders, and invites a "What's in it for *me*?" response

- *Goal as "vision"*: "supplant Citi!" – "Killing the competition" or similar goals may produce good short-term urgency, but will kill motivation stone-dead once the goal is reached

- *Marketing-slogan as "vision"*: "to be the best bankers of the century!" – This "to be the…" form combines every error: role-based, self-referential, goal-driven, spurious measure

It's unfortunate – to say the least – that that last error-example is the style actually *recommended* in many texts and standards, including the Business Motivation Model... Be warned, it does not work – it simply cannot do the job that a valid enterprise-vision needs to do.

Another visioning booby-trap that especially affects architects is *desired future-state as "vision"*: "our vision for the 'to-be' structure of the company." A future-state is effectively mission-as-vision, and it doesn't work as an enterprise vision. It's a bit unfair, because it's actually a subtle semantic problem – it's valid in its own way, but is a different meaning of "vision," and not vision in the sense we're using here. If in doubt, there's a simple test: if the "vision" describes something that is temporary, or narrow in scope – such as a typical "future-state architecture" – then it's not a vision that's usable for *this* purpose.

The participants divide up into small teams of four or five, and we split the remaining time into brief development-and-review cycles of ten to fifteen minutes each, to work toward something that resembles a usable vision.

To no one's great surprise, the first few passes provide several all-too-obvious examples of falling for every one of those pitfalls: a hyped-up "to be the best we can be!", for instance, or the dreary marketing-slogan "the best bank for you." Back we go, and back again, as the same mistakes get repeated time after time: and we begin to get worried, because it's looking all too possible that this group simply won't be able to get the point of the exercise – a way to reach *beyond* the usual self-centric marketing spiel, to something that will allow people to *connect* with the bank, and to re-create that respect.

Then out of the blue – or out of the welter of excitable slogans now scattered all over the walls – something usable at last appears: "better financial futures." It doesn't look much at first glance – it might not attract a marketer's eye, for example – but it *does* have the right feel, the right characteristics. What is it that interests *every* player in this shared-enterprise? Better financial futures. What is it that interests the government? Better financial futures. The bank? It wants better financial futures too. And likewise the customers, prospects, partners, suppliers, competitors, probably even the bank's enemies and anti-clients: *everyone*'s interested in better financial futures. It makes sense: it works. Or well enough for now, anyway – and much better than those marketing-slogans would have done so on their own.

Back in the workshop, we're now running out of time. Using that preliminary vision of "better financial futures," we skim through some quick examples that show how a vision would be used in business practice:

- *Customer relations*: Credit-card management and debt-reduction is not about stopping people from spending money, but about ensuring customers' better financial futures.

- *Internal operations*: Everything we do is about ensuring better financial futures throughout the extended-enterprise.

- *Government relations*: Our focus with government is around making better financial futures for the nation as a whole.

- *Risk management*: The purpose of risk-management is to ensure better financial futures.

- *Hiring policies*: We need people who are committed to creating better financial futures for everyone.

- *Community and philanthropy*: Our donations and support-schemes all revolve around better financial futures for the broader community.

And *now* we can come back to all the marketing-slogans and internal exhortations, to review each of *those* in terms of the vision. There are plenty of phrases up on that wall that – with perhaps a few tweaks here and there – would line up very nicely behind that feeling described by "better financial futures." Everything they've done so far still works: but they now have a clear reference-point against which everything and anything can be assessed. So it's now all starting to make sense: we can see the metaphoric light-bulbs lighting up behind many participants' eyes...

But at that point, it really *is* time to stop: time for a quick wrap-up, and then let them get on with the rest of their day.

Wrap-Up

We'd started from the problem of respect, or loss of it. From there we'd seen how respect was poor even within the organization, but more in a passive sense, that there was nothing to help tie them all together *as* an organization, and thence with their market and the broader community. So that's what we'd concentrated on: how we could link everything together.

You'll notice that we didn't mention "architecture" anywhere here – even though that's actually what this is.

That's why we'd started the workshop with the function-model, as a way to get everyone within the organization on the same page – literally so. Each member of the executive and senior-management could now *see* the part their own work played within the overall organization, where they overlapped with others, and where gaps in responsibilities might appear in future.

We'd then expanded that to show how the organization fitted in turn within the broader enterprise – the implied value-propositions and service-interfaces with every other player in the enterprise, including those stakeholders who might have no *direct* interaction with the organization.

And from there we'd moved on to the notion of a "vision," a single phrase that links every participant in the entire enterprise, both within the organization and beyond it. We'd shown how this differs from, say, a marketing-slogan, or from the usual business metrics. They themselves had found a usable starting-point for this – "better financial futures" – and we'd then explored how this could be used *in practice*, with immediate effect, and immediate practical impact.

Together, in effect, we'd created a space in which respect could exist: respect for each other within the organization, respect for the other players in the market and the broader enterprise, and also respect from those other players toward the organization and all the people within it. Sure, there's lot more still to do, to reclaim that respect, over the coming months and years: but the necessary foundations for all that work *are* now in place.

Quite a lot to have covered in a single morning, then.

As the participants file out of the room for the midday break, we grab the chance to make some quick notes for the following day's review with the change-manager; and then settle down to the quiet unnoticed slog of tidying up from the session.

Application

- How do you keep implementations "on track" to the architecture? How do you manage your relations with project-leads, portfolio-managers, solution-designers, and other implementation-folks? How do you avoid the dreaded role of "the architecture-police"?

- How do you engage with others to share that "one idea" that "things work better when they work together"? How do you explain to others that architecture and overall effectiveness are the responsibility of *everyone* in the enterprise? How do you bring others along with you on the "journey" that is enterprise-architecture?

- What are your own specialisms within architecture? To what extent are you a specialist in being a generalist?

- What, to you, is "the architecture of architecture"? How do you describe to others what you *do*? And what processes do you go through to improve your skills in the work that you do?

- What methods do you use for sensemaking and decision-making in architecture? How would you use those methods for sensemaking and decision-making about the architecture and practice of the architecture itself? What kind of meta-thinking and meta-methodology do you apply to your architecture?

- How do you identify the actual "problem" within any given context? How do you ensure that you have identified the "root cause" rather than a more surface-level symptom? What methods do you use for sensemaking and decision-making in unordered contexts where the concept of "cause and effect" may make little or no practical sense?

- How do you identify "solutions" for any given context? How do you limit the risk that a "solution"-option may constrain your view of the context? How do you align the overall "problem" with an appropriate set of "solutions"? By what means would you ensure that they remain aligned in the future? In what ways could you make your "solutions" self-adapting' to align themselves with any changes in the "problem"-context?

- What *patterns* do you note in sensemaking ("problem-patterns") or decision-making ("solution-patterns") in your own work? How would you describe those patterns? How would you validate them? How would you adapt and apply those patterns in practice within your architecture?

- How would you introduce "the architecture of the enterprise" to the executive and senior management of your own organization? What difficulties would you expect to have to deal with – especially with the "numbers-men" among them? How would you keep their interest engaged long enough for the practicality of these initially abstract ideas to start to sink in?

- How would you explain to your executive the difference between the organization and the enterprise – and that the broader-enterprise can never be under their control? How would you explain to them the impacts of the broader-enterprise on the organization, as expressed in themes such as respect, trust, or morale? How would you demonstrate the linkage between those seeming-abstract themes and their real impacts on the financial bottom-line? And how would you do so without touching on any "undiscussables" such as externally imposed business-policy?

- Architecturally speaking, how would you get everyone in the organization "on the same page"? How would you extend that beyond the organization, to include partners, suppliers, customers, the broader market, perhaps the broader community? What would be the advantages if you do so? Perhaps more to the point, what would be the disadvantages if you *don't* manage to do so? In what other architectural ways could you establish a unifying "totem pole for the tribes"?

Summary

In this chapter, we explored what happens – and needs to happen – as we move from plan to implementation. In the first of our two projects, we used the example of developing a new tool for architectural sensemaking – context-space mapping – to in turn make sense of the process itself. Architects are specialists in being generalists: we need the right tools and techniques to support that specialism. In the second project, we explored the step-by-step actions and outcomes of working on two capabilities that we needed the clients to develop for themselves: how to create a functional business model to aid in person-to-person communication across the organization; and a vision-statement that could help to "unify the tribes" and rebuild respect across the overall enterprise.

The main deliverables were, respectively, the descriptions and diagrams for context-space mapping, and new ways to make sense of the principles and practice of enterprise-architecture; and a functional-business model and vision-statement that the organization could put to immediate use.

In the next chapter, we'll review what we've done in those two parallel projects, and assess the value that's been gained from doing them.

CHAPTER 9

Day 9: What Did We Achieve?

By this point in the architecture-cycle, we would hope to have achieved something. But what *did* we achieve? With what benefits, and for whom? What can we learn from what we've done? And what should we do next?

So we here return to architecture-governance to do a "lessons-learned" review – a Retrospective, in Agile terms – in relation to the respective business context, and identify any needs for further related architecture work.

In a conventional large architecture-project, this would be a major phase in itself. The TOGAF standard, for example, treats it almost as a project in its own right, with the main aim of defining key themes for the next multi-year architecture-cycle. A more mature architecture environment would be able to run several projects in parallel, all at different speeds, with implementations varying from hours to years. For the mid-range, a separate review stage here may make less sense, and this part of the work may instead be done as part of a regular review meeting, perhaps once a month, adjusting the scope to assess whatever's been completed during that period. And when we get right down to the smaller scale, as in our examples here, it becomes best to lock the review to the respective architecture-cycle again, so as to ensure that the proper governance is applied in each case.

The "environmental-scanning" part of the work that TOGAF describes for here – assess changes in the business-environment, actual and potential developments in technology, and so on – still needs to be done, of course, together with the continual reassessment of the architecture itself. But in a more mature architecture-capability, that would typically be actioned as a distinct architecture-cycle in its own right, rather than patched onto other architecture-projects almost as an afterthought.

© Tom Graves 2023
T. Graves, *Everyday Enterprise Architecture*, https://doi.org/10.1007/978-1-4842-8904-4_9

So the review here should concentrate mainly on the specific business-problem with which we started this cycle. The "holographic" nature of the overall architecture always allows us to include the broader context, but as an automatic side-effect of that review rather than a somewhat artificial focus on what may well be a separate topic entirely.

Here the two types of governance – architecture-management and change-management – will need to come together to share the exploration and reassessment of what's been done. But while the governance may need to change a bit to suit the scale, the review-steps themselves are essentially the same in each case – and as usual, we need to keep it simple, and fast.

The basic theme throughout here is an "after-action review," which in essence comes down to just four questions that we apply again and again to each part of the work we've done to date:

- *What was supposed to happen?* – for which we need there to have been some kind of plan on which we would *act*

- *What actually happened?* – for which we need to have been able to *observe* what was going on, while it was going on

- *What was the source of any difference?* – for which we need to be able to *orient* ourselves and make sense of what was going on

- *What can we learn from this* – for which we need to be able to *decide* on possible changes to the way we think and work, and commit ourselves to those changes

---

Which, as you'll no doubt have noticed, is another variant of the OODA cycle, in effect offset by one half-step: we Decide what was supposed to happen; we Act, which makes things happen; we Observe what actually happened; we Orient ourselves to interpret the source of any difference; and we Decide what action to take, to change what should happen next time.

There are also two fundamental rules for an after-action review: "pin your stripes at the door," and "no blame." In essence, these are both about responsibility: whatever rank each person might have in their hierarchy, each had their own responsibilities, their own role to play; and we're here to learn, not to blame. Those two rules may not matter that much in the work we're doing in this specific context here, but they certainly do matter in the often-fraught, politicized contexts of most real enterprise-architecture: building those rules right into the core of architecture-governance really does help.

But on to our two projects, anyway.

Main Project: What Next for Our Architecture?

What was supposed to happen in this architecture-cycle? We'd set out with the aim to answer two specific questions:

- What do enterprise-architects *do*?

- How exactly do they add value to the business?

We also included a focus on speed of response, as one of the probable drivers for effective business-value. To demonstrate this, we gave ourselves a time-limit of just two working-weeks in which to contribute *something* useful toward answering those questions. The resultant *plan* could be summarized as follows:

- Use architecture ideas, models, and methods to describe how to do architecture-development, in real-time.

- The topic for the architecture-project is architecture itself.

- Document this in book-form, as text and images.

- Allocate a timescale of ten working days.

Our key references include the project-diary, the various diagrams and models, and any other notes we may have collected along the way. Overall, though, it's probably simplest to review this in terms of the respective phases of the architecture-cycle.

Phase A: Set Up the Architecture-Cycle

Back at the start, we quickly settled the more administrative items, such as the purpose – "improve understanding of how to work with the architecture of architecture" – and the stakeholders for the architecture-cycle – us, mainly – along with other themes such as time-horizons, level of detail, scope, and so on. Those were straightforward. Less straightforward was the awkward feeling of uncertainty – "I don't know what I'm doing" – which we resolved partly by sticking closely to the predefined process, and also just by doing *something* to break the initial inertia.

The "something" in this case was a brief wander around various ideas from other disciplines – in particular, a very close parallel with scientific investigation, which, as we saw, is itself more like an art or craft than a "science" as such. From that, we decided to include within the themes for this architecture-cycle rather more of an emphasis on "the technicalities of making the best use of the architect's mind" – particularly those aspects that deal more with "unorder" and uncertainty, with which architects clearly need to excel.

One side-theme that came up was the importance of holding back on any supposed "solutions" until the appropriate time – *not* during assessment, but only after all assessment is complete.

And other themes that were of note included that emphasis on the importance of improving architects' speed of response to clients' needs; on overall effectiveness rather than local efficiency; and the need for the architecture to be able to cover a whole-of-enterprise scope, rather solely that of a single domain or sub-domain such as IT. We also described architecture itself as "a body of knowledge about enterprise structure, story, purpose and value."

No particular "lessons-learned" there, probably, other than that it's not often that we can be explicit about how uncomfortable it is to deal with that initial uncertainty – but we *do* need to be honest about it, and not pretend that it doesn't exist.

Phase B: Assess the Primary Time-Horizon ("To-Be")

We'd previously decided to do the assessment "future-backward," starting with the "to-be" as the main focus for assessment. Again, this brought up quite a bit of that feeling of "spinning in circles, no traction, no place to start," but we dealt with it simply by getting started, by following the suggested steps for this part of the process. This led to a focus on sensemaking and decision-making, with architecture usually taking a decision-support role for others; and also on four sets of tools or concepts that we would apply throughout the cycle: five-domain context-space mapping, five-element lifecycle-model, five principles from systems-theory, and a "segments-model" rework of the classic Zachman framework commonly used in existing enterprise-architecture.

Using one of those systems-theory principles – recursion – we then used those four tools to look at what we needed from the "to-be" architecture-of-architecture, including the four tools themselves, and the skillsets needed for the work.

It's too early to describe any benefits as yet, though the main lesson-learned is the value of being able to wander off onto side-alleys as needed, yet still having a predefined plan to which we can return at any time if we start to feel lost.

Phase C: Assess the Comparison Time-Horizon ("As-Is")

The overall structures for architecture at present seemed much the same as in our "to-be"; the main difference was in scope. Almost all of present enterprise-architecture centers around IT, although some may also extend toward or include more of the organization as a whole. Very little encompasses the entire extended-enterprise – the scope we'd identified as essential for the "to-be" architecture. Yet so dominant is this IT-centrism that often, the only way to explain what enterprise-architecture needs to be is by describing what is *not* a valid enterprise-scope architecture.

It was also clear that at present there seems very little public awareness of the *actual* processes of architecture – moving beyond mere method toward meta-methodology and meta-thinking, the "thinking about thinking" that's essential to improve skills in practice.

The problems highlighted here can often be quite subtle, but their sheer scale is often a real eye-opener. Much of what passes for "enterprise-architecture" at present is little more than design for large IT-systems: the lesson-learned here is that there is still an urgent and mostly unaddressed need for a true "architecture of the enterprise."

Phase D: Assess Gaps Between As-Is and To-Be

Other themes that came up in the gap-analysis include the value of recursion within architecture itself, and a huge list of items to address that come up from a closer look at that notion of "the art of architectural investigation." From there, we noted also a need for our architecture to focus on overall effectiveness – indeed, that that theme forms a key part of the "value-proposition" for enterprise-scale architecture. But there are so many apparent requirements and options that we're forced to prioritize: the need to enhance the speed and, if possible, the accuracy of those "art-like" processes for making sense and making decisions in architecture would seem to come to the top of the bill here.

Probably the main lesson-learned here, again, is the usefulness of systems-thinking principles in architecture, both for sensemaking and for preliminary designs. But there's also the importance of avoiding "analysis-paralysis" – in this case, we did that avoidance by holding to a strict Agile-style time-box of a single day for the gap-analysis itself.

Phase E: Decide on What to Do About Those Gaps

Following the usual recommendations in the architecture-process, we did a literature-search, which turned up two likely candidates to match our requirements: the Observe-Orient-Decide-Act (OODA) cycle, and some of the underlying ideas from the SCAN framework. Neither of these could be used as a prepackaged "solution," but it did seem that, with some adaptation for architecture, the two could be merged together as a kind of "inner cycle" for sensemaking and decision-making, within the main architecture-cycle. There would still need to be a focus on speed – a focus which is already built in to OODA – and also to ensure that the implementation is fast, too.

The main lesson-learned here is that the most useful options for this purpose have all come from outside of architecture itself: a point we should certainly remember for other more mainstream applications of architecture.

Phase F: Develop a Detailed Action-Plan

What quickly became clear during this phase was that using those two items as simple checklists will not be enough: we'd not only need to merge OODA and the SCAN base-frame, but also show how to *use* them in architecture. The point here is that this was about "intangibles" such as the *feel* of architecture as much as it is about process and practice: we would need to find some way to get the balance right.

This brought us back to a focus on architecture as a generalist *skill*, and thence to a brief exploration of the tactics needed to support the development of new skills and techniques. The result was that our "action-plan" would be to use text and visuals to describe – or perhaps imply, or allude to – the kinds of skills needed in order to enhance our architecture. We'd also need practical examples, to bring these ideas down into usable form. Recursively, one of these examples would be this discussion itself. The other example would emphasize the point about the true breadth of architecture scope by using a real business-problem with whole-of-enterprise impacts.

One lesson-learned here, again, is that that uncomfortable feeling of uncertainty is both normal and *to be expected* at the start of this phase. Knowledge of that fact can help a lot to reduce some of the inherent stress of this stage... Another extremely important lesson is the reminder that not every context needs an IT-based "solution" – in fact may not need any "solution" as such at all. The challenge is always to find an *appropriate* answer to the needs of the context – and not try to force the context to fit whatever "answer" we may happen to have at hand.

Phase G: Execute the Action-Plan

For large-scale enterprise-architecture, the role in implementation will often only be in decision-support or compliance-management. In this case, though, the architecture had been the core of the implementation, using architecture itself to explore what architecture is, how it works, and what we need to do to make it work better, make it work faster. And the way we did that here was by exploring in more depth the process of sensemaking and decision-making that underpins every aspect of architectural skill.

Some of the themes covered in that exploration included sources for sensemaking; how to deal with inherent uncertainty; and how and why to hold back from making decisions too early. We also looked at different types of base-maps and cross-maps for different tasks in sensemaking; the importance of being clear which maps we're using at any time, and why; and the *dynamics* of "taking a walk" around these maps of context-space. Some of the base-maps also addressed specific themes such as business-architecture; there are other examples on this later in the book, in Appendix B. A further theme was on "problem-space" versus "solution-space," and the need to keep them apart until the moment of decision – hence those explicit boundaries between assessment and solution-design in the architecture-cycle.

Lessons-learned? It's difficult to say for certain, although reviewing the discipline of analysis and exploration has been useful in itself, I would hope. What's clear is that it *is* still remarkably hard to explain what it is that we do as architects, or how we actually do it. Whether this has been of practical benefit to your own architecture practice is something only you can decide, and perhaps only over a much longer timescale than one reading of a book.

Phase H: Review Our Progress So Far

Which, in yet another kind of recursion, brings us to here, the review of the review.

At this point, it'd be worth skimming back over those preceding summaries, to take note of the lessons-learned at each stage. Another item for that list would be the reminder of why this "meta-thinking" is so important to the discipline of architecture – and also that yes, it *is* hard work, much more difficult than it may seem at first glance.

Perhaps most important, though, is that the benefits need to be assessed not in terms of theory, but in how we apply it in our real-world *practice* – such as through using architecture to tackle that pressing problem of respect at the bank.

Example Project: What Next for the Bank?

We have a follow-up meeting booked for the following morning with our client, the bank's change-manager. He greets us warmly, and is evidently pleased to see us – always a good sign! We recorded his comments in the project-diary:

---

participants took key learnings from visioning into their strategy-session, became first real strategy-work they'd done in years
people really talking with each other – photos on function-model as literal conversation-starters
new focus on effectiveness across whole organization
"better financial futures" vision-tagline did act as anchor/focus for strategy-session

---

So yes, a lot of real value gained, he says. But he doesn't quite see how this links in with that initial theme of respect – which is still as serious a problem as before – and he also wants to know where it should go onward from here.

To explain all of this, we need to do a brief lessons-learned review, quickly skimming through all that we've done, step by step.

The original brief, in what became our *Phase A* for the project, was around the problem of loss of respect, affecting the whole organization from the outside at least. So the initial idea was to develop something that could help the executive tackle this, yet with the minimum possible disruption, as the organization was already over-stressed from "change-fatigue" after a recent merger. The change-manager could see the cultural issues and impacts, but the current CEO was essentially a "numbers-man" who showed little interest in how his organization actually worked as long as it could deliver the short-term results that he wanted. So our aim, as we'd agreed, was to set up a suitable high-level "architecture of the enterprise" that the change-manager could then leverage in subsequent work.

Working with him, we'd set up a couple of workshops – our *Phase B* – to gather information about the current context. What those indicated was that the problem of respect pervaded not only the organization's external relationships, but within the organization itself – a rather worrying "lesson learned" from that exercise. We'd then used architectural assessment techniques, such as POSIWID and five-element lifecycle-models, to identify and highlight some of the underlying systemic issues. From there, he'd given us the go-ahead for another brief exploratory session with selected staff, to gather further information about the current context, and the difference between past and present.

The results of that session, which again had some fairly painful "home truths" for our clients, became the basis for the "past to future" assessment – our *Phase C*. We had some good examples of what respect looked like in the past, and likewise its absence in the present. It quickly became clear that the conceptual *structure* of the organization was essentially unchanged between past and present; what *had* changed was policy, particularly a new near-obsession with "shareholder-value" from the parent-corporation. It was also clear, though, that this was an "undiscussable" issue: it had to be accepted as a "given." The only practical option would be to find another way round the issue while leaving the policy itself unquestioned, no matter how much damage that policy might cause. The most likely clue for action seemed to be that this was essentially about people's *feelings* in relation to the company and each other. As a *qualitative* issue, financial incentives or attempts at "control" would not work, but a more direct focus on feelings and commitments might have more success.

We'd reported on that to the client, and then turned to the gap-analysis – our *Phase D*. Given the unambiguous instruction to treat the policy problem as "undiscussable," we explored various other avenues of difference between past and present, of which the best prospect seemed to be the theme of collective *identity and unity* – a "totem-pole to unite the tribes." We'd done similar work in other organizations, and had found that the combination of a shared description of business-functions with a specific type of "vision-statement" would provide a common point of reference, enabling stronger respect for each other's work, and also providing a focus around which external respect could accumulate.

We then set up another brief meeting with the client to present our findings, and then discuss options for further action – our *Phase E*. We'd suggested that we could perhaps present a seminar on function-models and visioning for his change-management team; we were somewhat taken by surprise when he instead asked us to present it as a workshop for the full executive and senior management team – in just two days' time. The "lesson-learned" for us there was the necessity to be able to re-think an entire architectural approach at a moment's notice...

So we then had to adapt or develop a complete half-day workshop for executives, in just over a day – the only time available for our *Phase F*, the detail-plan stage of the architecture-cycle. Our usual structure for a workshop of this type would run for several days, and for a group of architects, not executives; but by applying some radical pruning we arrive at a session-design that would fit within the half-day timeslot that was available to us. A useful lesson here, perhaps, is that it *is* possible to strip away many of the conceptual items that we would usually regard as "essential," to derive that which really *is* the essence of that part of the architecture.

On to actual implementation and delivery – our *Phase G* – in a rather different role from the architects' usual one for this part of the architecture-cycle. And while we're eliciting the information needed for a high-level values-architecture for an organization, we're also in effect *teaching* the basics of whole-of-enterprise architecture to a somewhat special audience – creating engagement in these otherwise abstract ideas by making it *personal* for them with their own photographs and their own direct involvement. In the process of creating the function-model, there are key lessons about overlapping responsibilities, and other areas which have almost no mutual support – and the model also enables, and invites, new conversations across the enterprise by the simple yet literal fact of bringing everyone together "on the same page." The visioning process is challenging at times, but is likewise about *connecting* with other people, both within and beyond the organization. The key point here is that it's *not* about marketing as such – a point that did take quite some time to get across to the executive – but is again about creating *conversations*, a "conversation-*with*" rather than the usual marketing "talking-*at*." And through all of this, we still managed to avoid any of the "undiscussables," and even the term "architecture" itself – even though all of it was actually about the architecture of the enterprise.

Which brings us to this follow-up meeting – in effect, our *Phase H* review for this project. There are really two areas of focus here: the respect problem, and architecture in general. Although they're closely linked, it's probably best to keep them separate at the start.

The core of the respect-problem is the change in policy, to focus on short-term "shareholder-value" at the expense of almost everything else. This has huge yet often subtle knock-on effects, particularly in terms of damage to trust, which in turn impacts on respect. Yet no-one can even discuss this policy, let alone challenge it. For the bank, as a subsidiary of a much larger organization, that policy – however destructive – is effectively a strategic "given," almost as much as the laws of the countries in which they operate. So the only other option, such as described in economist John Kay's book *Obliquity*, is to come at it from some other direction.

The key here lies in what we sometimes describe as the "performance paradox": that we get the best performance in a given value by paying attention to everything *except* that specific value. It seems counter-intuitive at first, but as John Kay and many others have demonstrated, there's plenty of hard evidence to show that that it really does work that way. And it's actually what we *would* expect once we think in terms of terms of systems-theory rather than conventional linear analysis: the infamous "bottom-line" is a complex non-linear derivative from many non-reversible and non-replicable factors, which, in less technical terms, means there's no way to run the calculations backwards *from* the desired bottom-line result *to* any of the factors that we can actually control.

So, for example, to get the best financial return, we need to keep the focus on something *other* than financial-return. Hence one of the main reasons for choosing to emphasize enterprise-vision: it provides exactly that kind of focus that we need here, a central reference-point around which all of the key factors that feed into that bottom-line will naturally coalesce. Within the organization, *internally*, the vision provides a consistent yardstick against which we can assess whether anything and everything is "on purpose" – which, in turn, will drive the bottom-line.

The other key point is that the vision is perhaps even more about *external* contacts: it gives people a *reason* to start a conversation with the company, and also, again, gives a clear test for others as to whether the company is "on purpose." And it's from those conversations that the desired respect – and, in turn, those needed transactions – should ultimately arise.

So there's plenty of work right there for our client and his change-management team. The vision becomes the central anchor for a *values-architecture* that needs to pervade the entire organization: every metric needs to align with the vision, for example; every item of marketing; every aspect of training; all bonus-structures and performance-measures, for teams and for individuals. The only area, in fact, that would *not* need to be touched by this is the final financials: which means that, this way round, we *can* safely leave those "undiscussables" undiscussed.

On the other side, the work on the function-model, we suggest that it would be well worthwhile to extend that exercise quite a bit further, to fill in the remainder of the tier-2 overview and make a solid start on the tier-3 detail. Our experience elsewhere has been that a function-model diagram that's fully populated at tier-3 has huge and immediate value throughout the business, as a tool for coordination and communication across all of the silos, and also for planning and project-management. We've seen it used for training, too, to show new staff where their work fits within the whole. We've even seen it used for cost-management, and cost-based prioritization of change-projects. Overall, it's one artefact that immediately *sells* the idea – and the value – of architecture to the business in general.

Yet even more, as with the vision, it's a tool for *conversations*. It places everyone on the same page – literally. When it's physically large enough – as in our example – we can attach photographs or other items that *personalize* that picture, instantly enabling a more direct and *human* level of communication between people. And that kind of connection brings enormous returns, in time saved, in problems avoided, and in improvements in the general ease and flow everywhere across the organization. All of which eventually flows downward into the bottom-line.

What happens next? Well, that's up to the client in this case: we're only external consultants. But there's a lot of work there that could be of huge value to them, as they can see: and we'll be glad to help in that, any way that we can.

Application

- How do you review the value of your architecture work? In particular, how do you identify benefits realized and lessons learned?

- How do you describe and demonstrate to others those benefits of that architecture-work – especially if the benefits are not tangible, or cannot be described in simple monetary metrics?

- What do you learn in this review-process? What challenges or changes does it suggest, for the architecture, for your own skills or actions, or those of others? What actions do you take on any lessons-learned? How do you ensure that you enact any commitments to change that arise from those lessons-learned?

- How do you engage your clients and other stakeholders in these review-processes? What do you each learn from this? Perhaps especially, what do you learn about architecture by working with people who are *not* architects?

- What happens when the architecture plan needs to change at a moment's notice? How do you manage the sense of confusion and disorientation that arises from this? How quickly can you re-think your overall plan? What do you need available to you in order to do so?

- If you're used to working with system-designers, project-managers, and other architects, how does it feel when you're suddenly asked to present to a group of executives? In what ways does the story need to change, and why? How does the architectural story change with other audience-groups too, such as operations-staff, or vendors, or business-partners and other direct peers?

- How do you demonstrate the linkage between architecture and key business issues? In particular, in what ways would you use the architecture to resolve those key business problems while safely sidestepping any "undiscussables"?

Summary

In this chapter, we explored how to do an after-action review, and how to make use of the information gathered from that review. We went step-by-step through both projects, identifying the outcomes and lessons-learned from each phase of the respective project. The "Application" section at the end of the chapter provided questions to help you adapt those principles and practices for use on your own organization's context.

The main deliverables from this chapter were the notes taken during the reviews, and the list of suggested follow-up actions.

In the next chapter, we'll apply the same kind of review to the broader project of this book as a whole.

CHAPTER 10

Day 10: What Happens Next?

We now need to start the wrap-up for the whole project: identify benefits and lessons-learned, and decide what to do next. As in the wrap-up for the two sub-projects, it's probably simplest if we follow the structure of the After Action Review (Figure 10-1):

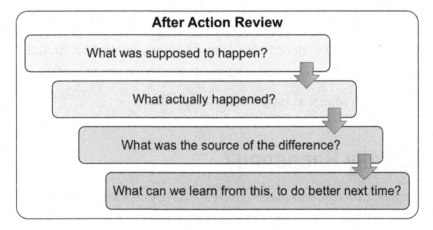

Figure 10-1. *After Action Review*

What Was Supposed to Happen?

The questions with which we started were

- What do architects do?

- And how do architects add value to the business?

Which is rather too large a scope to attempt to tackle in one go: but we could do so by looking at the underlying principles, and then finding ways to illustrate

© Tom Graves 2023
T. Graves, *Everyday Enterprise Architecture*, https://doi.org/10.1007/978-1-4842-8904-4_10

those key principles. So, from this, we derived a set of commitments for a brief architecture-project:

- Use architecture methods and related methods to describe how to do architecture-development in real-time.

- Topic for the architecture-project is architecture itself.

- Document in book-form.

- Timescale of ten working days.

We then added a bit more detail, deriving the following summary of key themes and understandings about what the item of work would involve and should achieve:

- Project-stakeholders are architects and architects' clients.

- Use the existing Agile-architecture development-process.

- Demonstrate the recursion and suchlike within that process.

- Particularly want to describe the sensemaking and decision-making components of architecture, such as via context-space mapping.

That, in effect, was what was supposed to happen here.

What Actually Happened?

We did use *architecture-methods* to describe various key aspects of enterprise-architecture, in what was effectively a simulation of real-time work – subject to constraints imposed by the book-style format.

To address the topic of "*architecture itself*," we actually ended up doing three projects in parallel:

- An overview, describing the architecture-process, which became the introduction to each day's chapter.

- The "main project" example, which described the architecture principles being used in that day's work.

- The "example project," a somewhat fictionalized compilation from several real-life architecture assignments, which we then used to illustrate how those principles apply in real practice.

So, for the purposes of this exercise, those three actually form sub-projects or layers of the same overall project – in effect also illustrating the point about recursion.

This is, as you can see, *documented in book-format*. The *text-style and content* were *aimed at enterprise-architects* and, especially, for other architects who might want to explore the enterprise-architecture domain. Although some of it was fairly theoretical, it should still make sense for most strategists, project-managers, and others who work with a larger-scale scope – in other words, the typical clients for enterprise-architecture. So that part was in accordance with the plan, too.

We did also *use the existing Agile-architecture development-process*. This was loosely based on the well-known TOGAF Architectural Development Method (ADM), but adapted for a more Agile-type style, explicitly iterative and recursive, and usable for *any* scope. We demonstrated part of this *recursion* with a cycle that contained an embedded second cycle, which itself included two further sub-projects.

We wanted to emphasize the processes of *sensemaking and decision-making* in architecture, using methods such as *context-space maps* that describe the natural layering, recursion, and reflexion within enterprise-architectures. We've probably achieved this, with two fully worked examples and upward of 50 diagrams, though perhaps still with not quite enough explanation as yet of the real *dynamics* that apply in the use of context-space maps. But it's enough with which to get started, we would hope.

The *timescale of ten working days* was probably realistic enough for this purpose. The real work described in the two sub-projects in fact took less than that – particularly the "bank example," whose real-world components were compressed into barely half of that time. (In our own work, we've done complete architecture-cycles in as little as two hours, rather than the two weeks allowed here – though that didn't include much of an implementation, of course. But this here is still a *lot* faster than the two-years-to-business-benefit usually expected for a classic TOGAF-style architecture-cycle...) The writing took rather longer than ten days – almost three times as long, in fact – though that was somewhat to be expected, for reasons we'll explore in a moment.

Some other key themes that came up during the work:

- The generalist and eclectic nature of architecture-work

- The real difficulties of working with inherent uncertainty

- The centrality of systems-thinking in making sense of deep-uncertainty

- The fundamental distinction between organization and enterprise

- The enterprise comprises *people*, so person-to-person communication really matters here

- The enterprise not only *has* a story, but *is* a story

- The role of architecture in identifying and promoting that story

We had several reminders throughout this period that architecture is necessarily *generalist and eclectic*. Most of architecture is about decisions of some kind; and many if not most of those decisions are emotional at root, about feelings and "gut-feel," a sensitive awareness of tendencies and trends. It's about "big-picture," about finding common unifying-themes within the ways that everything connects with everything else. Which means that we need a good understanding of how everything connects with everything else – which in turn leads to the need to be generalist and eclectic in our approach to architectures.

Architecture, design, and engineering are all closely related, but have different concerns, different emphases, different approaches to any given context. Engineering will focus on the fine details, on the tangible, the concrete, on that which purports to be "objective," on "things." Architecture will emphasize overall scope and scale, the intangible, the *feel* of things, the subjective, the connections *between* things. And the role of design is to bridge the gaps – hence architects need design in order to realize their ideas, and engineers need design in order to make their work usable and to connect with the work of others. Engineers and the like can usually remain specialists throughout their careers; but architects *must* be generalists, to link across all of those specialist domains that make up their respective "world."

The point here is that many business-folk – perhaps most – have a mindset that is closer to that of the engineer than the architect: the specialist rather than the generalist. *Someone* in the business must hold the generalist view, and in principle that's a key part of the role of the CEO. But as we saw in the bank example, the CEO may also be solely a specialist, a "numbers-man" in that case. Somewhat bizarrely, the only person there who maintained the generalist view was our client, the change-manager – but he didn't have the authority to do much within that role. This kind of situation is not unusual in large organizations, and is a common source of serious enterprise problems: so architects, as some of the few generalists around in the business, can often find themselves placed in the awkward role of arbitrator between warring specialists. It's another way in which the job can become "relentlessly political" – as one of my colleagues put it – and another reason why we'll *definitely* need strong "people-skills" to do this work well.

The relentless politics of business, important though they may be, are only one of the sources of *inherent uncertainty* in architecture. We came across a lot of this during this worked-exercise, particularly at the start of each phase, where that sense of "I-don't-know-what-I'm-doing" will often hit hard for a while. That feeling can be uncomfortable in the extreme: but it *is* part of our role as architects to work with it, in order to find the designs and structures and solutions that we need. And it *is* also a normal part of the work, hence should be no surprise – in fact is actually a sign of *success* – whenever we come across it again.

During this cycle, we had several reminders that *systems thinking* is one of the most valuable approaches to architecture, and one that will often also help in dealing with that inherent uncertainty. It's especially useful in navigating through the "uncertainty" domains – particularly the Ambiguous, perhaps less so in the Not-known.

Note that the type of systems-thinking referred to here is what's sometimes known as "soft-systems theory," which particularly relates to human systems. There's a quite different type called "hard-systems theory," which is more about feedback loops and delays, and which more properly belongs in the extreme end of the Complicated domain. It's important not to confuse the two approaches, because they work in very different ways: for example, hard-systems theory assumes repeatability – in principle, at least – whereas soft-systems theory doesn't.

We started out looking at enterprise architecture, but quite soon came across the *fundamental distinction between "organization" and "enterprise"*: an organization is bounded by rules, but an enterprise is bounded by values. Failing to grasp this distinction was a key source of problems for the bank, for example: they'd viewed their market and the broader enterprise as an extension of their own organization, and hence as something subject to their "control" – which it wasn't. And the enterprise itself comprises people, hence *person-to-person communication* really does matter – both in the bank-example, and also throughout our own architecture.

Finally, *the enterprise has and is a story* – for which the core of that story is the enterprise vision. And as we've seen, architecture has a fundamental role in identifying that story, in linking it to the structures and purpose of the organization, and in promoting that story throughout the enterprise as a whole.

What Was the Source of the Difference?

The aim was to use architecture methods and related methods to describe how to do real architecture-development in real-time. And the topic for the architecture-project was architecture itself; and the intent was to document all of that in the form of a book – this book. The stakeholders for all of this were architects, and clients of architects; and we did follow the defined Agile-style architecture development-process. All of that we did indeed achieve here: no real difference between plan and execution.

The production of the book did take a fair while longer than the nominal ten days – just under 30 days from start to finish, in fact. The reason for the difference is that all of this does take a *lot* longer to write than it does to say… And although the intent had been to use hand-drawn diagrams, to convey the immediacy of the real-time work, the idea unfortunately didn't work in practice – all of the diagrams needed to be redrawn to make them more readable within the much tighter space-constraints of the printed page. It is true, though, that all of the actual architecture work *was* completed within the stated time: ten working days, one day per stage, exactly as shown here.

There was a lot more repetition and revisiting of the same themes than is usual in this kind of book. I'll admit that, as a writer, this amount of repetition can feel somewhat disconcerting at times, but it does seem to be required by the nature of the work itself – iterative, recursive, re-entrant, reflective. We often arrive back at what may *seem* to be the same place, yet each time it's from a different direction, and with a slightly different view – hence adding more detail, more depth and richness, to the holograph-like map of the enterprise.

Another theme was that while a conventional textbook would follow a standard order and structure, here our aim is to illustrate the *uncertainty* of architecture – which, almost by definition, must sometimes force us into somewhat strange places. The standard architecture-process is usually described as a Simple sequence of steps, but the moment we touch the real world, those steps – and the process itself – will soon become Complicated, Ambiguous, and even Not-known. And that *is* how it should be – otherwise it wouldn't be much use in the real world. Much of the *process* of architecture is inherently uncertain – and there are real difficulties that arise from that fact. Likewise the *results* of that architecture-process are always somewhat uncertain: we should know beforehand what we aim to achieve, but that really *is* almost the limit of our control over the results themselves. If there isn't at least *something* that's unexpected, we probably aren't doing architecture. In that sense, the development of the architecture-story here does reflect the sense of *inevitability* of uncertainty and ambiguity – even though that structural uncertainty was not part of the original project-plan.

The bank-example was also not part of the original plan. It soon became obvious, though, that the project needed a concrete real-world example of the *use* of these ideas and themes, rather than only one that should make sense to experienced architects but perhaps be too abstract for other people elsewhere in the business. This extra example added another facet to the overall layering within the project, yet without disrupting the intended timescale – a definite bonus.

There's one aspect of sensemaking with context-space maps that may not have been adequately covered here, namely, the *dynamics* of sensemaking. "Go for a walk around the map" is a good overall summary of what happens, but perhaps not enough to describe the way in which the focus and even the mindset will change – and *need* to change – as we move around within that conceptual space. The tactics that we use in the Simple domain, for example – sense what's going on, choose an option from a checklist, and act on it straight away – are crucially different from those we need to use in the Not-known domain, which will often oscillate wildly from the old "don't just stand there, do something!" to a more Zen-like "don't just do something, stand there!" so that the new information that we need can arise in its own way and time. Yet this is not at all easy to describe in words: it does seem, unfortunately, that it *is* one part of architecture that's so personal that it's best explained through experience alone.

What Can We Learn from This?

Two themes seem to stand out:

- The importance of following the process
- The subtle strength of the *parti*

The eight-part process we've used here was originally designed for the relatively narrow scope of IT infrastructure-architecture; but in this more iterative, layered form, it will work well for *any* scope, and for any scale. Yet the same recursion described *by* the process also necessarily applies *to* the process itself: it isn't just a step-by-step tick-the-boxes checklist, but instead must likewise wander round within its own context-space map. So in practice, that all-important instruction "follow the process" may have many different meanings:

- *Simple*: For best practice in known contexts, do it "by the book."

- *Complicated*: When more factors are involved, we may have to stop for a while to analyze our options, perhaps repeating some steps to define good practice in this specific context.

- *Ambiguous*: When the context becomes inherently uncertain – such as with "wicked problems" – we need to use experiments, often running in parallel, to allow appropriate practice to emerge.

- *Not-known*: When there is no clarity of direction at all, work with the Open Space concept that "whatever happens is what is meant to happen," and permit new ideas and new practices to arise from the "no-thing-ness" of extreme uncertainty.

This is where architects' experience comes into the story, because we need to know how to "walk around" among these domain-views of the process in order to *use* the process in architecture. The process becomes a context-space map of itself, which we must then use *as* a context-space map to help us to use other context-space maps – a lovely example of the kind of extreme recursion that's all too common in architecture-work. And trying to explain that kind of recursion to others, without sending their heads spinning, is *not* easy at all: that's probably one of the less-helpful lessons from this overall exercise. Must Do Better Next Time, perhaps? But this *is* the process, however chaotic it may seem at times – and we do need to follow it as best we can, wherever it may lead us in the end.

In contrast, the architectural notion of the *parti* is one of the most useful items that came out of this exercise. In some ways it's like a "solution," though not a solution as such – more an architectural motif that arises seemingly from nowhere, yet acts as the constant mirror against which everything else is reflected. Importantly, it's likely to turn up right at the start of the architecture-cycle, at that moment where we've understood the project-brief and make the first move outward from "the unknown" into a subtle, almost-chaotic space where, for a very short time, it seems that anything and everything could be possible. That motif is often only visible for one fleeting moment, so we need to allow ourselves to become quietly aware of it – which is rarely easy in the circumstances. But if we can allow this *parti* to appear, it makes all of the work much, much easier, because it acts as a central unifying theme around which all other information and ideas can coalesce.

In his book *The Secrets of Consulting*, the great computer-industry consultant Gerry Weinberg alludes to the same kind of motif occurring in consultancy-practice. Whenever he goes on an assignment, he says, "I always get the answer in the first five minutes" – though it can often take him hours, or days, or weeks, to recognize what it was that he saw in those first five minutes…

In one example in that book, the first blurted greeting by a young staffer was a near-frantic "How can *you* get away without wearing a tie on business?" – the problem in that company turned out to be excessive formality, sticking to the rules even when the rules didn't work.

One of my own best examples was from many years ago now. It was in a trouble-shooting job for a typesetting bureau: the stench of film-developer chemicals literally slammed into my nostrils as soon as I opened the front door. The company was excellent in its handling of the computing side of the business, but slapdash in almost anything to do with the physical world – which meant that much of their output was ruined by poor-quality film-processing and the like. "I get the answer in the first five minutes": one of the most valuable lessons I've ever learned in consulting – and in architecture too.

The *parti* in this case, for example, was that tag-line that came up almost at the start of Day 1: "things work better when they work together, with clarity, with elegance, on purpose." *Everything* here has in some way been about purpose, about being on-purpose, about clarity of purpose. It's certainly been true of the worked-example of sensemaking and decision-making; and especially so for the bank example, because, as we saw, respect is intimately interwoven with clarity of purpose – hence, in their case, the importance of that focus on vision and purpose.

But it's also important to note that the *parti* is not a solution: it's more about a *feeling* or focus or overall direction, rather than some kind of explicit action. That initial feel of the *parti* is often right, but initial ideas about implementations usually aren't – which is why we *must* take care to shelve all would-be "solutions" until the time *is* right to look at our options for implementation. And while the feel of the *parti* will usually remain much the same throughout the process, its outward form may change a lot – hence the iterative nature of so much of architecture-work, over and over, turning and returning, watching carefully while the details of the picture subtly change around the constant core of the *parti*.

These are the "lessons learned" that I've derived from this overall exercise. What you've found will no doubt be somewhat different, because each of us comes at the work from our own background, our own specific experiences, and each of us will learn in our own different ways.

Yet for all of us, there's always more to learn – *always*. In some ways, that's the whole point of architecture, really: to create, and to learn. And to find new ways to make things work better, work together, with clarity, with elegance, and on purpose.

Application

- How do you review your own work? What formal processes or checklists do you use for this? In what ways could you improve those review-processes, and for what benefit to you and others?

- What did you expect from this book? What actually happened for you while reading this book? If what you discovered while reading the book was different from what you expected, what was the source of each of the differences? What can you learn from these differences, to change how you approach a similar context in future?

- In what ways did you expect this book to change how you view your own work-context? What actually happened to the way you now view that context? What actually happens *in* that context as a result of any changes in the way you view it? What was the source of each difference? And what can you learn from this, to change the way you work – and your approach to that work – in the future?

Summary

In this chapter, we again explore the use of an after-action review, this time applied to the book-project as a whole. This presents a further illustration of how architectures can and often must change as we go through from initial idea to assessments to plan and final implementation. The "Application" section at the end of the chapter provides questions to help you apply this in your own work, and to review what you've learnt throughout this book.

The main "deliverables" for this chapter are the changes in your own view and experience of architecture and architecture-practice.

APPENDIX A

The Architecture Information-Stores

We've described enterprise-architecture as maintaining a body of knowledge about enterprise structure, story, purpose and value – which means that there'll be a lot of data, information, and artifacts to manage somehow! The key information-stores we would need to maintain are

- Architecture-governance repository.

- Architecture-models repository.

- Requirements repository.

- Issues, dispensations, risks, and opportunities registers.

- Glossary and thesaurus.

We haven't described much about these during this project, but it'd be worthwhile to have a brief look at what they are and how they would be used in a more typical architecture scenario.

Architecture-Governance Repository

This store keeps track of everything and every activity that would, should, and has happened during architecture work. Most of this should be set up in Phase A of the architecture-cycle, and then maintained and updated as required as the cycle progresses.

© Tom Graves 2023
T. Graves, *Everyday Enterprise Architecture*, https://doi.org/10.1007/978-1-4842-8904-4

In a simpler environment this could be a straightforward spreadsheet, or perhaps even an ordinary handwritten project-diary, as in the example-projects here. But as soon as we lift toward any more significant work, we'll need something significantly more sophisticated. Some of the purpose-built enterprise-architecture toolsets have built-in project-tracking facilities; otherwise any of the software tools for problem-tracking or for Agile-style software development will do the job, though perhaps with a few tweaks here and there to fit better with this type of work. Most of the usual tools for project-management probably won't fit so well for this, though: they tend to assume a linear or Waterfall form of project-lifecycle, whereas this type of work, as we've seen, will often demand a process that is looser and more freeform in its approach – yet still remain under known governance every step of the way.

Governance here is not about control – although it can sometimes be misused that way – but more about support for responsibility and for shared-learning. For example, we can't usefully ask the question "What was supposed to happen?" unless we have some idea – and preferably some record – of the initial plan; and we can't ask "What actually happened?" unless we have a record of that too. Another key point here is that these items should also identify the "who" of each project – all the stakeholders who need to be engaged and informed, and who often provide the essential pieces of otherwise missing information that we'll need to make a project work. Recording the activities at each stage may at times seem a bureaucratic nuisance, but being able to search quickly through records of past work has often saved us many hours of frustration: it *is* well worth the effort.

Architecture-Models Repository

Models and diagrams are probably the most visible output of the architecture trade, although it's important to remember that they may have almost no value in and of themselves: their real purpose is as aids for *communication* about architectural ideas, designs, and implementations. All of the purpose-built "enterprise-architecture" toolsets can churn out any number of models, and will store the structures for them within some kind of internal repository; yet they often forget to mention that those models are not actually the architecture itself...

There are several key exceptions to the "these are only of interest to architects" guideline above, of which perhaps the most important are the core vision and the set of functional business models and/or capability-maps (see the example-project section in the Day 8 chapter for more on this). These, and a few other types of models, really do need to be available to everyone, as they're likely to be used almost everywhere throughout the organization.

Most of the architecture-models will be created in Phases B, C, and D, although solution-architects and designers will also produce many of their own in Phases E and F. For simple work, we can often get by with Visio and the like, or with a recording-whiteboard or a sketchbook: it doesn't need to be anything fancy, as long as it *does* support that task of communication. That's all we used for the examples here: they all started out as rough sketches, and were only "cleaned-up" on Visio for this published version because the handwritten text was too rough to be readable as-is.

Note too that it's not just the models themselves that we maintain in this type of information-store, but also notational standards, metamodels, and even meta-metamodels – the structures for the structures for the final models that will describe something real. Most of the diagrams for the main project here have been metamodels and the like, while there've been rather more of the ordinary models for the bank-project example.

Requirements Repository

This repository is a structured catalogue and store for all kinds of requirements that may come up during architecture work. Most of the architecture-specific requirements would come up in Phase D of the architecture-cycle, from the gap-analysis, but other types of requirements may come up literally at any time.

There's an unfortunate tendency, among developers in particular, to think that requirements are merely project-specific. This is true of some requirements, of course, but very much not all: laws, standards, and non-functionals such as security and safety may impose some very real requirements across multiple, many, or even all projects.

This repository should probably be maintained by the portfolio or project office, but it *must* be curated and aggregated across all projects, and *must* be accessible for quick, structured search by architects, because otherwise there's no way for them to identify gaps, overlaps, duplications between projects, or assist in reducing technical-debt and the like. Most purpose-built requirements-management software will include support for those kinds of searches as a standard function.

As before, a simple spreadsheet may be adequate for the earlier maturity-levels of architecture work. As the scale and the scope broaden, though, so too does the complexity of the relationships between the requirements, and a purpose-built tool soon becomes all but essential.

The list should also include any constraints – which in principle are a kind of externally imposed requirement – and linkages to all manner of other items such as business-rules, business decisions, strategies, policies, and applicable regulations. There may be many types of relationships between these items, such as "‹implements›," "‹extends›," "‹conflicts with›," and so on. For architecture, *every* requirement should ultimately link back to that core requirement for the enterprise itself – the vision.

Issues, Dispensations, Risks, and Opportunities Registers

We use these registers to record a variety of themes that are not requirements as such, but may well lead to requirements or other actions. We always track risks and opportunities as a matched pair, because they're flip-sides of each other: opportunities always imply risks, and risks should also always imply opportunities, if we think about that for a while. As described earlier, dispensations are a special-case of architectural risk, in that they represent risk that we've allowed ourselves to take on for pragmatic reasons, but which will need renewed review whenever we touch the respective scope. What we call "issues" are in effect the remaining items that don't fit into either of those other categories. The relation-types between these items include "‹amplifies›," "‹extends›," "‹resolves›," "‹impacts›," and so on. We may come across these in any phase of the architecture-cycle, but particularly in the assessment-stages, in Phases B, C, and D.

Another term you may come across for this is "RAID log" – an acronym for a register of risks, actions, issues, and decisions. In essence, that's the same sort of thing that we're talking about here, though we've partitioned it somewhat differently: for example, "actions and decisions" would be more likely stored in the Architecture-governance repository rather than in this one. The big difference is that conventional risk-registers rarely include opportunities and their linkage with risks, whereas for architecture-work support for those is an often-essential requirement.

We haven't covered many risks, opportunities, or the like during the projects here: the various ideas for "solutions" in the early phases were effectively a type of opportunity carried over to the later design-phases. And that "undiscussable" bank policy that assigned extreme priority to "shareholder-value" was another example where we needed to record a dispensation about a problem with serious yet unavoidable *architectural* risks for the enterprise. In small projects such as these here, we could record these items as entries in the project-diary; but a spreadsheet or small database would still be a better option, and integration into a proper purpose-built toolset better still.

Glossary and Thesaurus

Although these haven't featured in either of our example-projects, the combined glossary and thesaurus is one of the most important architectural documents: communication across the enterprise could be almost impossible without it. The kind of technical terms that we would record in this will need to be tightly linked to architectural models – so much so that some purpose-built toolsets will generate a basic glossary automatically from the models-repository. But it's essential that the two items are closely coupled, because the thesaurus makes little sense without the definitions in the glossary, and ambiguities and alternatives for key terms in the glossary are often only visible when linked with the thesaurus. Relationships between items would include "‹use›," "‹use-for›," "‹broader-term›," "‹narrower-term›," "‹related›," and "‹unrelated›." These last would be references to items that might appear to be related but are actually different, with diverse meanings from different contexts, such as a formal standard, or a descriptor for a business unit, or a software application, all with the same or similar-seeming term. We would typically identify these items during the assessment stage, particularly in Phase B and C, but may also come across them elsewhere in the cycle.

A spreadsheet or record-book will not really be enough for this: the glossary and thesaurus really *do* need to be published, and in an easily accessible form, to make them available to everyone. For example, some of our clients have had great success with a "jargon-buster" lookup on the home-page of an intranet. Ideally, it should be possible for anyone to suggest new terms, new definitions, and especially new cross-references for the thesaurus, because that alone can prevent much interdepartmental confusion and many painful arguments about the "real meaning" of specific terms. A wiki or some other simple user-editable online tool can also be of real benefit here – especially one such as the free Wikimedia software which can also do "sounds-like" searches for ambiguous, half-remembered words.

Application

- What information do you store on architecture-governance, models and metamodels, requirements, risks, opportunities, dispensations, and other issues? How and where do you track definitions and cross-references between key terms?

- How do you store and manage that information? Who has access to create, read, update, and delete any items, for what reasons, and under what governance?

- In what ways do you associate specific stakeholders with certain items of information, and for what reasons?

- How do you maintain that information? In particular, how do you keep it up to date? What version-management, archiving, migration to new host-systems, and suchlike do you need to apply, especially over the longer-term? What processes and governance are applied to ensure that this is done?

- In what ways will these need to change as you expand the architecture to a full enterprise-wide scope?

APPENDIX B

More on Context-Space Mapping

To make sense with context-space mapping, we first need to go right back to first-principles: the core concept of context-space.

Before any notion of order or structure, there is simply "the everything": everything and nothing, all one, with that "everything-and-nothing" linked to everything-and-nothing else, in a place-that-is-no-place that incorporates within itself every possibility. It's not "chaos" – it simply *is*. That's always where we start.

There are all manner of names for this "active no-thing-ness." Lao Tse called it "the Tao," for example, while the ancient Greeks described it as "the Void." In many of the diagrams here, I've used the term "*reality*" as the center, to remind us of this. Yet for the more business-oriented purposes of enterprise-architecture, though, we'll need to constrain the scope of that "the everything" somewhat, into a smaller subset of that reality, a narrower and more usable chunk of context. So let's call that *context-space* – the holographic, bounded-yet-unbounded space that still contains every possibility within that chosen context (see Figure B-1).

Figure B-1. *Context-space*

Elsewhere in this book, I've split this context-space into *problem-space* – the context in which things happen – and *solution-space* – the space in which we decide what to do in relation to what's happening. But ultimately there's just the context: "the only true model of a system is the system itself."

© Tom Graves 2023
T. Graves, *Everyday Enterprise Architecture*, https://doi.org/10.1007/978-1-4842-8904-4

Yet to make sense of anything, we need to impose some kind of structure. One place to start would be to filter "the everything" in terms of its variability. Perceived-repeatability is one obvious example of a variability that we might find useful, but there are of course many others.

At the start, this gives us a finely graded spectrum of variability across the context (see Figure B-2).

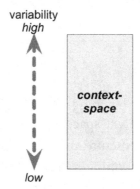

Figure B-2. *Variability in context-space*

Interestingly, though, most human sensory-perception does not work well with smooth gradations: it works much better with firmer boundaries. Hence most sensemaking will usually attempt to place some kind of ordered structure upon what may initially seem like unbounded chaos, to act as a filter that can help us to separate "signal" – that which we're interested in – from "noise" – that which is not of apparent interest for now *(see Figure B-3)*.

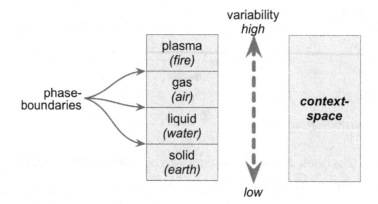

Figure B-3. *Phases of variability in context-space*

For example, when we look at the physical world of matter and material, we can see both of these processes in action, even within matter itself. There is a fairly smooth gradation of variability, primarily linked to temperature; yet there are also explicit "phase-boundaries" where the internal relationships of matter undergo fundamental changes. Significant amounts of energy ("latent heat") can be absorbed or released in the "phase-transitions" between these modes. In effect, these will present as four distinct states of matter, traditionally described as Earth, Water, Air and Fire, for which the respective scientific terms are Solid, Liquid, Gas and Plasma (see Figure B-4).

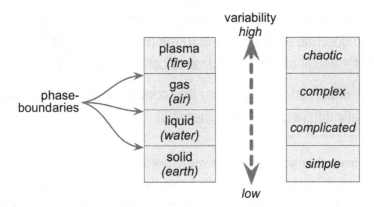

Figure B-4. *Phases as domains of context-space*

When we look at the *internal* structures of matter within each of these states, we would typically describe the respective structural relationships as simple, complicated, complex, and chaotic, as phases or domains within the context-space of matter. This type of categorization along a single axis represents a simple first-order map of that context-space – hence *context-space mapping*.

We can do the same with almost any other gradation-type view into that overall context-space. Within that gradation, we should be able to identify, or choose, phase-boundaries that partition the context-space into distinct regions along that axis: for example, the nominal split of the visible-light spectrum into red, orange, yellow, green, blue, indigo, and violet.

For enterprise-architecture, business-architecture and the like, maybe the most useful split is along an axis of repeatability, dividing the inherent uncertainty of context-space into regions that, in parallel with those states of matter, we could perhaps describe, respectively, as Simple, Complicated, Complex, and Chaotic.

There's a risk at this point that some people might mistake this for the well-known Cynefin framework.

Given that risk of confusion, it's *really* important to note that what we're describing here is *not* Cynefin. The two frameworks might look somewhat similar at the surface, but they are different in many fundamental ways: they have different origins and a different theoretical base, they are used in significantly different ways, and they have different roles and functions in the overall process of sensemaking and decision-making. To illustrate the difference, context-space mapping would describe a Cynefin-style frame (though not Cynefin's methods!) as merely one instantiation of a generic class of context-space base-maps.

Once again, it's important to understand that context-space mapping and Cynefin are fundamentally different: don't mix them up!

For our purposes, though, there's one more tweak that we need to make on terminology, in order to reduce possible misinterpretations in sensemaking. Simple and Complicated are both safe enough as terms: they both fit cleanly into a simple cause–effect world, so we can safely leave them unchanged. But as terms, Complex tends to be complex, and Chaotic often downright chaotic: there are way too many meanings for both of these. For example, "Chaotic" can mean anything from the colloquial chaos of "I have no idea what's going on here," to the mind-bending complexities of quantum-mechanics and chaos-science. To simplify these right down, we'll swap "Complex" for the unambiguous term "Ambiguous," and "Chaotic" for the term "Not-known" – because the latter is most often what we're dealing with in everyday chaos. Overall, that gives us an acronym of SCAN: Simple, Complicated, Ambiguous, Not-known. We'll also use the term "Reality" to denote any part of the context where we haven't yet sorted anything out into usable categories.

With that terminology issue settled, we can also see

- How and why we've arrived at those particular categorizations

- How and why to use any specific axis for such categorization

- What the boundaries between the "domains" in the categorization will look like

- How, why, and when the nominally Simple boundaries between categories may move around (Complicated), blur (Ambiguous) or fragment (Not-known)

This provides us with a layered, recursive richness that is largely absent in most other sensemaking-frameworks. It also provides a means to link right across every possible view into context-space, rather than solely a specific set of interventions that focus only on a single domain.

A first-order (single-axis) context-space map – such as the Simple-to-Chaotic "stack" in Figure B-4 – is not all that much use in practice. To make it more useful, we'll often need to add other axes as filters for sensemaking, to enable relevant information to fall out of the respective comparison. And we make it more useful again by selecting a related set of axes to provide a multi-dimensional base-map upon which other filters can be placed.

Simple two-dimensional base-maps are the easiest to work with, for obvious reasons, but three or more dimensions are entirely feasible – the tetradian (see Figure 8-9 or 8-10) is one example of a four-dimensional frame compressed into three-dimensions for use as a base-map.

To do this, we choose axes that force the domains of that original single-axis spectrum into relations of opposition and similarity with each other. For example, we could use "levels of abstraction" as the core axis, and overlay that with timescale in one direction and a "value-versus-truth" spectrum in the other. As shown in Figure B-5, that would give us the respective base-map and its "cross-map" of interpretive text-overlays:

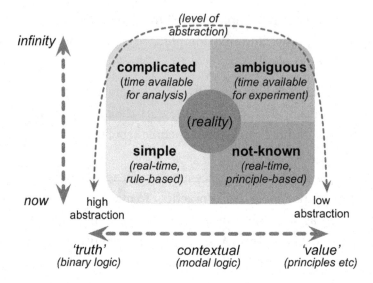

Figure B-5. *Context-space: abstraction, interpretation, timescale*

Here Simple and Not-known are opposites in their interpretations, but similar in terms of timescale; Ambiguous and Not-known are similar in their means of interpretation, but opposites in terms of timescale; Simple and Ambiguous, and Complicated and Not-known, oppose each other on both axes; yet all domains are related in terms of layers of abstraction. The central region of Reality is essentially a reminder that all of the other domains are each just an abstraction from the real: they represent related yet arbitrary views into what is actually the total "hologram" of the context-space.

We then layer this recursively to apply to the nominal boundaries between each of the domains, so that these too may be considered to be fixed, movable, blurred, or porous, or fragmented, or transient. An axis based on a binary "true-or-false" categorization (in other words, a Simple boundary) will split the context-space into two domains along that axis. If both overlay-axes have Simple categorizations (or movable two-part categorizations, in Complicated style), the overall context-space is split into four regions – which aligns well with the "matter"-type categorization of Simple, Complicated, Complex, and Chaotic back in Figure B-4. Likewise a smooth gradation along both axes pushes the context-space into four regions with Ambiguous or even chaotic Not-known boundaries between them.

Because of this, a four-region base-map is likely to be the most common and most useful two-dimensional type. Other layouts are possible, of course, and often useful: for example, a pair of tri-value axes would typically be used to align an eight- or nine-domain primary axis, such as seven-color plus infra-red and ultra-violet.

The result is a consistent structure for base-maps that are both bounded *and* not-bounded, and that describe the whole of a context-space by structured views into that context-space that also acknowledge that, in reality, the context-space itself has no actual structure.

SCAN Cross-Map (Response-Patterns)

So far there are well over a hundred SCAN cross-maps for use in enterprise-architecture assessments. Figure B-6 presents one such example of a cross-map for sensemaking:

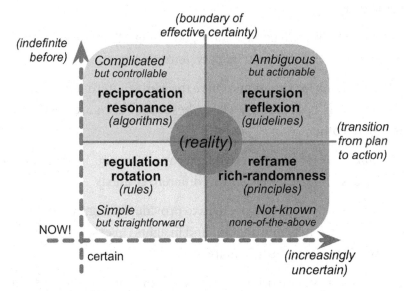

Figure B-6. *SCAN keywords cross-map*

This shows three cross-maps on the SCAN base-frame:

- Typical governance-methods in each of the domains ("algorithms," etc.)

- Keywords for typical tactics to use with each of the four main domains ("reciprocation," etc.)

- The core axes for SCAN dynamics ("Now!", "certain," etc.)

The *governance-methods* are straightforward: we would typically use rules for anything that's currently "in" the Simple domain, algorithms for anything that's "in" the Complicated domain, and so on. (The bit about "in" relates to SCAN dynamics, which we'll see in a moment.)

The *tactics-keywords* are suggestions for how to tackle assessment of something that's currently "in" the respective domain:

- *Rotation*: Work our way through a list, such as a set of work-instructions or a checklist.

- *Regulation*: Follow the rules and guidance of an existing standard or regulation.

- *Reciprocation*: Look for balance across interactions within the overall system.

- *Resonance*: Look for feedback-loops, damping-effects, and similar characteristic patterns from hard-systems theory.

- *Recursion*: Look for situations where the same pattern repeats at different levels – particularly where these repetitions are nested inside each other.

- *Reflexion*: Look for situations where a pattern repeats in "self-similar" form across multiple levels and/or different contexts.

- *Reframe*: Use multiple perspectives to provide different views in a context, to elicit new information and insights (in essence, this is what we do in context-space mapping).

- *Rich-randomness*: Use principles as "seed-anchors" to elicit insights from structured serendipity and suchlike.

The *SCAN dynamics* arise from the two axes of the framework, and how they interact:

- *Vertical-axis*: Amount of time remaining before action must be taken, working backwards from the "NOW!"

- *Horizontal-axis*: Level of uncertainty or uniqueness in the context, from "certain" to infinitely uncertain or unique

- *Transition from plan to action*: Moving downward toward the "NOW!" a relative and mobile marker to indicate the moment at which we run out of time to plan, and must begin to shift into action; in essence, the point after which stopping to think will slow things down

- *Boundary of effective-certainty*: Moving side to side, a relative and mobile marker to indicate the level of uncertainty that can be tackled within the current context

The point about "in" a domain is that things move around. For example, as a project moves from plan toward execution, we have to simplify it down to a form that we *can* execute – especially if we want it to execute fast. That means we'd be shifting from Complicated to Simple – which then means that Simple rules and governance would apply. If we have to go back to plan, everything slows down. If things go wrong in execution, we'll find ourselves in the Not-known domain – and will need to follow the tactics for that domain to work our way back to Simple again. You'll also see another example in action in the next cross-map, about idea-development. Things move around in sensemaking, as we build our understanding of those things, so the tactics we use at each moment need to change and move around with them.

Jungian-Type Base-Map ("Embodied Best-Practice")

The next cross-map, in Figure B-7, draws on Jungian concepts to explore the sequence of idea-development:

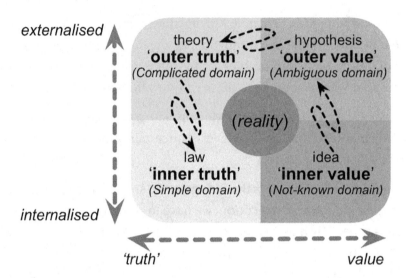

Figure B-7. *Idea-development*

This again illustrates the concept of "movement" within the categorized context-space. The idea first arises in and from the Not-known aspect of the context. At the start, it only has "inner value" – it exists only within that person, and it has not yet been tested. We then put the idea out for test: it becomes "real"-enough to describe to others, where it gains some level of "outer value," though for the while it still remains Ambiguous. Once the idea has coalesced as a more concrete hypothesis, it slowly migrates toward the Complicated domain, becoming "outer truth," a tested and usable theory. After further refinement, the theory becomes internalized as "inner truth," a "law of science" or suchlike that underpins Simple, certain practice. Throughout all of this, there's usually a lot of jostling back-and-forth between domains, as the levels of certainty and so on get settled out.

Ideally, the sequence should become a full loop, with Simple "law" feeding new ideas in the Not-known – but unfortunately, once an idea becomes "law," it tends to get stuck there forever, preventing further innovation even when necessary. In such cases, innovation may become possible only via a transit through the region of "Reality," shredding the categories and assumptions back to the raw basics – which in a business context can be disruptive in almost every possible sense…

Repeatability and "Truth"

This is a straightforward cross-map, in some ways taking us back to the core concepts of SCAN. It's also one example where it might make more sense to show the domains as a vertical stack (see Figure B-4).

As shown in Figure B-8, a Simple world requires a close correlation between repeatability and truth – or, as in most of the sciences, something can be considered "true" only if it is repeatable. The further we move away from that correlation, the more we are forced to move into the other domains, and thence into the different tactics that each of those domains requires. A flurry of special-cases becomes Complicated; things that repeat only some of the time are definitely Ambiguous; and things that barely repeat at all, or ever, would certainly throw us into the Not-known. Most real-world contexts incorporate a mix of all of these: hence why we need to be able to identify which domain we're dealing with at each moment, and switch our tactics immediately to match.

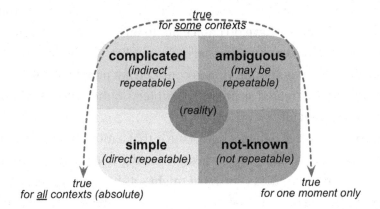

Figure B-8. *Repeatability and "truth"*

Marketing Versus Sales

Figure B-9 provides a useful cross-map that explores the perennial clash between Marketing and Sales. This draws on that dimension of timescale, from infinite to immediate, and on a less commonly used yet perhaps more important dimension: the concept of ownership, across a spectrum from *possession* – the default view in modern societies – to *responsibility* – which is actually more common in practice within organizations themselves.

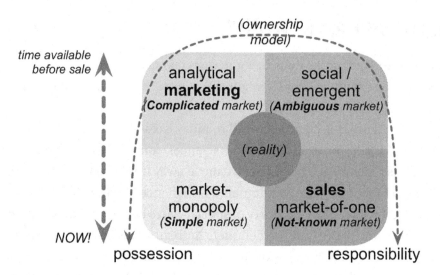

Figure B-9. *Marketing versus sales*

The most Simple market is a monopoly. You alone set the rules, and others (particularly the "consumers") have no choice but to buy according to your rules. In an all-too-literal sense, you *possess* that portion of the market, and hence also that portion of people's lives. Much of it is about trying to control what people do, often in a very physical sense: people are treated as objects or subjects rather than *as* people, and there is no need for marketing at all.

Yet there are two very real dangers here. One is that a monopoly is an extreme abstraction of reality, and if reality moves away from alignment with that purported "truth," the market can sometimes vanish overnight – as happens quite often on the Internet, for example. The other is that monopolies often breed deep-seated resentment, and if the monopoly cannot be bypassed, the resentment may explode elsewhere – as happened with British monopolies on salt, fabrics, and many other essential items in colonial India. We see much the same in lesser form with Microsoft's current dominance of the operating-system and office-software markets – contexts where a "natural monopoly" will tend to occur simply because of the need for standardized information interchange. So while possession of a market may *seem* like the best possible strategy, the long-term consequences can be much riskier than they look.

Most conventional marketing sits firmly in the Complicated domain: crunch the numbers, map the trends, analyze every-which-way to find out how to make the market predictable. People tend to be regarded as units of information, a datapoint within the statistics, rather than as individual people; in fact, it's very much about information, the conceptual dimension, and often also about trying to "control" what people think about a product or service. Trying to determine what people feel pushes the emphasis more toward the Ambiguous domain, while the common notion here of "taking control" of a market pushes the emphasis the other way, toward the Simple domain and all of its concomitant risks. Note also the cross-map with timescale: marketing may occur *before* or *after* but not *at* the exact moment of sale.

We move into a more Ambiguous domain of marketing in any emergent-market, or whenever we regard people more *as* people rather than as "consumers." This type of market demands much more acceptance of human factors, of "wicked problems" and other real-world forms of complexity. Often there will also be a need for a weakening of the separation between "us" ("producers") and "them" ("consumers") – as can be seen in co-operatives, in some forms of crowdsourcing, and also in Agile-type development where the customer is also part of the development-team. The central theme is about relationships, which, although still "abstract" in terms of timescale, may in effect extend and push the boundary of this domain quite a long way toward real-time, into what would otherwise be Not-known space.

Yet by definition, Sales themselves will always reside in the Not-known domain, because every decision to buy or not-buy is in part a quantum-event, a "market-of-one." The ultimate drivers for all such decisions are values-based, not "rational" or "truth"-based, which means – as just about any good salesperson would tell us – that the focus here is on emotion, on *aspirations*. And given that sales deals with real-time events, we're somewhat forced into the principles-versus-rules spectrum there (see Figure B-6). Online sales will go toward the rule-based end of the spectrum, because that's all that IT systems can handle; but real salespeople working face-to-face with real clients or customers (not "consumers" here!) will recognize key principles such as the need to listen – and also to know when to stop talking, so as to allow space for the decision to take place.

This cross-map also shows us that, by definition, the conventional approaches to sales and marketing are diametrically opposed by the nature of what they do and how they work. Yet we can bridge that gap somewhat either via the Ambiguous domain of emergent marketing, or else by the Simple-domain methods such as IT-based sales – though supported, again, by cross-links to Ambiguous-domain tactics to remove the risk and resentment around perceived monopolies. Which approach is "best" in each case will depend on the context – which this cross-map, and others, will again help us to identify.

Plan/Do/Check/Act

Figure B-10 shows another very useful cross-map that helps to clarify what's actually happening within the PDCA improvement-cycle, and is also a good illustration of the *dynamics* in context-space mapping.

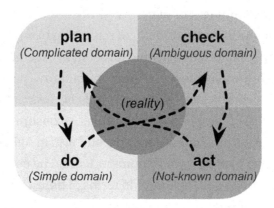

Figure B-10. *The Plan/Do/Check/Act cycle*

The cycle starts with Plan. This is primarily about information, and takes place before real-time contact, both of which tend to place it in the Complicated domain.

The aim of the Plan is to create rules that are Simple enough to apply in real-time when we Do the actual work. Although "work" can take many forms, it still needs to be made concrete in some way in the real world, which in effect places an emphasis on the physical dimension.

The work itself is not abstract: it happens in the real world, in real-time – in other words, it requires a transit through the inherent uncertainty of the undefined Reality domain.

On completion, we move back out of real-time to reflect on the difference between what we'd intended in Plan and Do; what actually happened during that transit through real-world Reality; and what we can do about it, in Check, and leading onward to Act. Learnings need to be both personal and collective, which places us on the "values" side of the "truth"/"value" spectrum (see Figure B-7). Long-term experience indicates that such learning takes place in a social or relational context, away from the action, through tactics such as After Action Reviews – all of which indicates that this part of the cycle situates in the Ambiguous domain.

The outcome of the Check phase is a set of guidelines for revised future action. We need to Act on those guidelines so as to embody the required changes in personal awareness and action, via a personal review of the underlying principles of the context and how they apply to that specific individual. To change how we work also requires that we face the personal challenges implied by any kind of change, so it's also about personal aspirations and personal responsibility, in the sense of "response-ability" – the ability to choose appropriate responses to the context in real-time action. Ultimately all of this is unique to the individual, a "market-of-one" (see Figure B-9) – and hence places this phase of the PDCA cycle in the Not-known domain.

We then wait for an appropriate new real-world context – in other words, another transit through "Reality" – to start the cycle again with a new Plan.

This cycle is also echoed in the problem-solving method first proposed by the Hungarian mathematician George Polya in his 1945 classic *How To Solve It*. The steps in his cycle are: Understand the problem; Devise a plan; Carry out the plan; Review and extend – which is the same as PDCA, but starting one step earlier, where PDCA's "Act" includes a re-understanding of the problem.

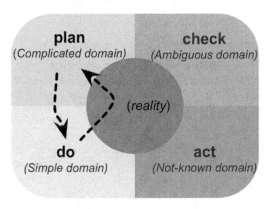

Figure B-11. *Failure-path – Plan/Do loop*

There are several ways in which the PDCA cycle can fail. One is that an obsessive production-oriented context skews the path to take a shortcut through Reality, to give a tighter loop of Plan/Do/(Reality)/Plan (see Figure B-11). This cuts out Check and Act – which may seem unnecessary in the short-term, but is probably disastrous in the medium- to longer-term, since it assumes that the rules created by the plan will always apply. Not so much Simple as dangerously simplistic...

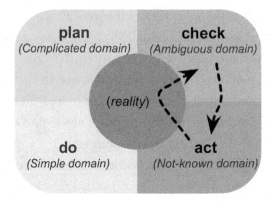

Figure B-12. *Failure-path – Check/Act loop*

Another type of failure occurs when extreme self-doubt skews the other return-path back through Reality to give a probably even-tighter loop of Check/Act/(Reality)/Check (see Figure B-12). In effect, this is a kind of personalized version of "analysis-paralysis" – much may be learned, but nothing is actually done, because the loop never arrives at Do.

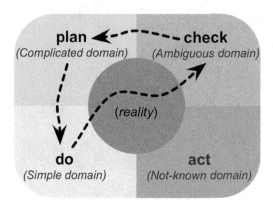

Figure B-13. *Failure-path – Plan/Do/Check loop*

Yet another failure-loop is Plan/Do/(Reality)/Check/Plan, in which the review takes place, but pressure of work forces a return to the Plan phase before any actual change can be embedded in personal action via Act (see Figure B-13). This is perhaps the least effective form of "process-improvement," but seems depressingly common in real-world business-practice.

ISO-9000 Core

The ISO-9000 core (vision, policy, procedure, work-instruction) provides a fairly straightforward cross-map to something that's usually presented as a vertical stack, but actually makes more sense in a base-diagram layout (see Figure B-14).

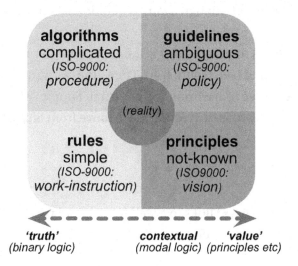

Figure B-14. *ISO-9000 cross-map*

A *work-instruction* defines Simple rules that apply to a specific context. In segment-model terms, it provides the row-4 or row-5 detail-level What, How, and Who that apply at a specific When-event, with Where usually defined in more generic terms (such as any location that uses a specific machine). The underlying Why is usually not specified.

When anything significant needs to change – for example, a new version of software, or a new machine – we move "upward" to the *procedure* to define new work-instructions for the changed context. This accepts that the world is more Complicated than can be described in simple rules, yet is still assumed to be predictable. The procedure specifies the Who in terms of responsibilities, and also far more of the underlying Why – the row-3 "logical" layer, in segment-model terms.

When the procedure's guiding reasons and responsibilities need to change, we move upward again to *policy*. This provides guidance in a more Ambiguous world of modal-logic: in requirements-modeling terms, a more fluid "should" or "could" rather than the imperative "shall." The policy describes the Why for dependent procedures – the row-2 "conceptual" layer, in segment-model terms (though "relational" might be a more accurate term here, as we'll see from other cross-maps).

When the "world" of the context changes to the extent that the fundamental assumptions of current policy can no longer apply, we turn to *vision*. This is a core set of statements about principles and values that in effect define what the enterprise is. Because this vision should never change, it provides a stable anchor in any Not-known context – in segment-model terms, either the row-1 "contextual," row-0 "enterprise" layers or "universals" segment (though again "aspirational" might be a more useful term here).

Note that in some ways this cross-map is the exact opposite of the "Repeatability and truth" cross-map earlier (see Figure B-8). There, the purported "universality" of a given "truth" increases as we move from Not-known to Simple, whereas here the values become more general and broader in scope as we move from Simple to Not-known.

Skill-Levels

This cross-map (see Figure B-15) links to a well-known and very useful heuristic on the amount of time that it takes to develop specific levels of skill.

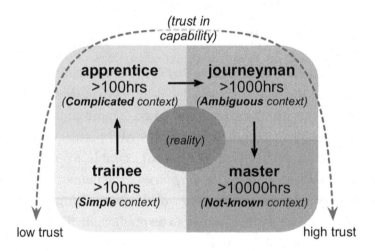

Figure B-15. *Skill-levels*

The "trust in capability" spectrum here is actually an inverse of the amount of supervision needed both to compensate for lack of skill and to shield the person from the consequences of real-world complexity and chaos in that context.

A *trainee* can be "let loose" on Simple tasks after about ten hours or so of disciplined practice (a 1–2 day training-course).

An *apprentice* will begin to be able to tackle more Complicated tasks after about 100 hours of disciplined practice (2–4 weeks). However, most of those tasks will still need to be supervised, and insulated from real-world complexity.

A *journeyman* will begin to be able to tackle more Ambiguous tasks that include inherent uncertainties after some 1000 hours of disciplined practice (six months full-time experience). Typical uncertainties include variability of materials, slippage of schedules, and, above all, people. Traditionally there is an intermediate point within the 1000–10000 hour range at which the person is expected to go out on their own with only minimal mentoring: in education, this is the completion of the bachelor's degree, while in a traditional technical training, this is the point at which the apprentice becomes qualified as a literal "journeyman" or "day-paid worker."

A trainee should reach a *master* level after about 10,000 hours (five years) of disciplined practice. This was the traditional point at which a journeyman was expected to produce a "master-piece" to demonstrate their literal "mastery" in handling the often-chaotic Not-known nature of the real-world. This period is also still the typical duration of a university education from freshman to completion of master's degree.

Skill should continue to be developed thereafter, supported by the peer-group. Building-architects, for example, often come into their prime only in their fifties or later: it really does take that long to assimilate and embody all of the vast range of information and experiences that are needed to do the work well. Hence, there is yet another heuristic level of 100,000 hours or so (more than 50 years) – which is probably the amount of experience needed to cope with true Reality.

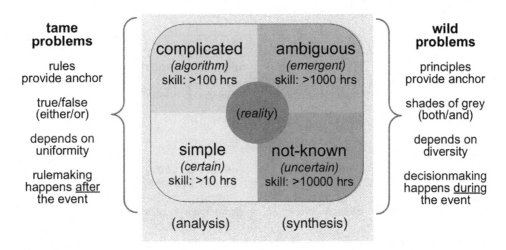

Figure B-16. *Skills, problem-types, and decision-making*

Another skills cross-map (see Figure B-16) shows why this isn't as straightforward as a simple linear stack. In the earlier stages of skills-development – from Simple to later Complicated – we in effect pretend that each context is predictable, controllable, reducible to some kind of ordered system. Up until the end of that stage, we only face predictable *tame-problems*, for which *analysis* alone is usually enough.

But at some point, late in the apprenticeship, there's a crucial transition beyond which we need to be able to tackle *wild-problems* that may be unique, unrepeatable, or inherently uncertain, and require *synthesis* as much if not more than analysis. These are real-world challenges that we can learn to *direct* what happens, yet it can never actually be *controlled* – a distinction that is sometimes subtle but extremely important, and actually marks the transition to true skill. This is where we must make the move toward the skills of the journeyman, to tackle the Ambiguous, and onward to the deep-skills of the master, to tackle the unique and the Not-known.

As indicated in the cross-map above, there are *fundamental* differences in worldview on either side of that transition. To tackle the full complexities of Reality, analysis alone is not enough.

Automated Versus Manual Processes

This final cross-map on automation (see Figure B-17) is a logical corollary from the skills-maps above (see Figures B-15 and B-16). It also has cross-links with the asset-types set (see Figure 8-9). The cross-map itself is reasonably straightforward, but also has extremely important implications for systems-design.

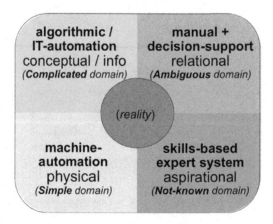

Figure B-17. *Automated versus manual processes*

Physical machines follow Simple rules – the "laws of physics" and the like. The Victorians in particular did brilliant work exploring what can be done with mechanical ingenuity – such as Babbage's "difference engine," or, earlier, Harrison's chronometer. Yet, in the end, there are real limits to what can be done with unassisted machines.

Once we introduce real-time information-processing, algorithmic automation becomes possible, capable of handling a much more Complicated world. Yet here too there are real limits – most of which become all too evident when system-designers make the mistake of thinking that "complexity" is solely a synonym for "very complicated."

As with skills-development, there is a crucial crossover-point at which we have to accept that the world is not entirely repeatable, and that it does include inherent uncertainties. One of the most important breakthroughs in IT-based systems here has been the shift to heuristic pattern-recognition – yet there are real dangers, especially in military robotics, that system-designers will delude themselves into thinking that this is as predictable as it is for the Complicated contexts. Instead, to work with the interweaving relational interdependencies of this Ambiguous domain – especially the real complexities of relations between real people – the best use of automation here is to provide decision-support for human decision-making.

In a true Not-known context, by definition there is little or nothing that a rule-based system can work with, since – again by definition – there are no perceivable cause–effect relationships, and hence no perceivable rules. The only viable option here is a true expert skills-based system, embodied primarily in a real person rather than solely an IT-based "system." These would rely on principles and aspirations to guide real-time decision-making. One essential point is that there is no way to determine beforehand what any decision will be, and hence how decisions are made. Although there are indeed a very small number of IT-based systems that operate in this kind of "world" – such as those based on "genetic-programming" concepts – we have no real certainty at the detail-level as to how they actually work!

Note that most – perhaps all – real-world contexts include a mix of all of these domains. This is why any real-world system must provide appropriate procedures for escalation and de-escalation: moving "upward" from Simple to Ambiguous to handle inherent-uncertainty via human skills, and "downward" from Ambiguous to Simple to make best use of the reliability and predictability of machines.

APPENDIX C

Resources

Books and Publications

Tetradian Enterprise Architecture Series

Tom Graves, *Real Enterprise Architecture: beyond IT to the whole enterprise* (Tetradian, 2008) – describes a high-level framework and method for whole-of-enterprise architecture

Tom Graves, *Bridging the Silos: enterprise architecture for IT-architects* (Tetradian, 2008) – describes how to adapt and extend IT-architecture *de facto* standards such as Zachman, TOGAF, FEAF, ITIL and PRINCE2 for use at a whole-of-enterprise scope

Tom Graves, *SEMPER and SCORE: enhancing enterprise effectiveness* (Tetradian, 2008) – describes a suite of tools and techniques to enhance enterprise effectiveness, such as the SCORE extension to SWOT strategy-assessment, and the SEMPER diagnostic and metric for enterprise effectiveness

Tom Graves, *Power and Response-ability: the human side of systems* (Tetradian, 2008) – describes the business implications of the dichotomy that while the physics definition of "power" is "the ability to do work," most social definitions are closer to the ability to avoid it

Tom Graves, *The Service Oriented Enterprise: enterprise architecture and viable systems* (Tetradian, 2009) – describes how to extend the principle of service-oriented architecture to the design and structure of the entire enterprise

Tom Graves, *Doing Enterprise Architecture: process and practice in the real enterprise* (Tetradian, 2009) – describes business-driven architecture, developing the organization's architecture capability in line with a defined, measurable maturity-model

Tom Graves, *Mapping The Enterprise: modelling the enterprise as services with the Enterprise Canvas* (Tetradian, 2010) – demonstrates how to map out services, service-relationships, value-flows, coordination, and governance consistently out to any scope and scale

T. Graves, *Everyday Enterprise Architecture*, https://doi.org/10.1007/978-1-4842-8904-4

Tom Graves, *The Enterprise As Story: the role of narrative in enterprise architecture* (Tetradian, 2012) – shows how stories underpin every aspect of the enterprise, and how to use story within the architecture to enhance enterprise effectiveness

Tom Graves with Joseph Chittenden, *Change-mapping: connecting business tools to manage change* (Tetradian, 2020) – presents a systematic method to guide change at any scope and scale, across every type of content or context, and for any timescale

Tom Graves with Joseph Chittenden, *Tools For Change-mapping: expanding the Change-mapping toolkit* (Tetradian, 2021) – provides a suite of plug-in extensions to the standard Change-mapping toolkit to cover a broader range of more specialized needs

Tom Graves with Joseph Chittenden, *Advanced Change-mapping: exploring, resolving and addressing issues of any size and complexity* (Tetradian, 2022) – shows how to expand Change-mapping practice to tackle enterprise-scale challenges

Other Books and Publications

WIB Beveridge, *The Art of Scientific Investigation* (Heinemann, 1950)

Matthew Frederick, *101 Things I Learned In Architecture School* (The MIT Press, 2007)

Tom Graves, *Inventing Reality* (3rd ed.) (Grey House, 2007)

John Kay, *Obliquity: Why our goals are best achieved indirectly* (Profile Books, 2010)

The Open Group, *TOGAF™ Version 9* (Van Haren, 2009)

Alex Osterwalder, Yves Pigneur et al., *Business Model Generation* (OSF 2010)

Georgy Polya, *How to solve it: a new aspect of mathematical method,* (2nd ed., Doubleday Anchor, 1957)

Gerald M Weinberg, *The Secrets of Consulting: A guide to giving and getting advice successfully* (Dorset House, 1985)

Websites and Other Online Resources

Business Model Generation (Business Model Canvas): www.businessmodelgeneration.com/ and www.slideshare.net/Alex.Osterwalder/business-model-canvas-poster

Business Motivation Model: www.businessrulesgroup.org/bmm.shtml

DyA (Dynamic Architecture): eng.dya.info/Home/

Pragmatic Enterprise Architecture: www.pragmaticea.com

TOGAF (The Open Group Architecture Framework): https://publications.opengroup.org/standards/togaf/specifications /

Wikipedia

All of the following Wikipedia references should be prefixed with `http://`
`en.wikipedia.org/wiki/`*.*

After Action Review: After_action_review

eTOM (Enhanced Telecom Operation Map): ETOM

FEAF (Federal Enterprise Architecture Framework): Federal_Enterprise_Architecture

Group Dynamics: Tuckman_Model or Forming,_storming,_norming_and_
performing

Kanban: Kanban and Kanban_cards

OODA cycle: OODA_loop

Open Space techniques for collaboration in complex contexts: Open_Space_
Technology

Polya's "How to Solve It": How_to_Solve_It

SCOR (Supply Chain Operations Reference): SCOR or Supply-Chain_Operations_
Reference

CP Snow's "The Two Cultures" (the arts and the sciences): The_Two_Cultures

Index

A

© Tom Graves 2023

T. Graves, *Everyday Enterprise Architecture*, https://doi.org/10.1007/978-1-4842-8904-4

R